WERE YOU THERE?

The Bishop Henry McNeal Turner/Sojourner Truth Series in Black Religion

Editor: Dwight N. Hopkins
  The University of Chicago, The Divinity School

Associate Editors:
  James H. Cone, Union Theological Seminary, New York
  Katie G. Cannon, Temple University
  Cain Hope Felder, Howard University, School of Divinity
  Jacquelyn Grant, The Interdenominational Theological
     Center
  Delores S. Williams, Union Theological Seminary, New York

The purpose of this series is to encourage the development of biblical, historical, theological, ethical, and pastoral works that analyze the role of the churches and other religious movements in the liberation struggles of black women and men in the United States, particularly the poor, and their relationship to struggles in the Third World.

Named after Bishop Henry McNeal Turner (1843-1915) and Sojourner Truth (1797?-1883), the series reflects the spirit of these two visionaries and witnesses for the black struggle for liberation. Bishop Turner was a churchman, a political figure, a missionary, and a pan-Africanist. Sojourner Truth was an illiterate former slave who championed black emancipation, women's rights, and the liberating spirit of the gospel.

Previously published in the Turner Series

1. *For My People* by James H. Cone
2. *Black and African Theologies* by Josiah U. Young
3. *Troubling Biblical Waters* by Cain Hope Felder
4. *Black Theology USA and South Africa* by Dwight N. Hopkins
5. *Empower the People* by Theodore Walker, Jr.
6. *A Common Journey* by George C.L. Cummings
7. *Dark Symbols, Obscure Signs* by Riggin R. Earl, Jr.
8. *A Troubling in My Soul* by Emilie Townes
9. *The Black Christ* by Kelly Brown Douglas

In the Turner/Truth Series

10. *Christianity on Trial* by Mark L. Chapman

The Bishop Henry McNeal Turner/Sojourner Truth Series
in Black Religion, Volume XI

David Emmanuel Goatley

WERE YOU THERE?

Godforsakenness in Slave Religion

ORBIS BOOKS

Maryknoll, New York 10545

The Catholic Foreign Mission Society of America (Maryknoll) recruits and trains people for overseas missionary service. Through Orbis Books, Maryknoll aims to foster the international dialogue that is essential to mission. The books published, however, reflect the opinions of their authors and are not meant to represent the official position of the society.

Orbis/ISBN 1-57075-063-7

To W. H. and Lillian
for faith

To Pamela
for love

To Atiba Emmanuel
for hope

Were you there when they crucified my Lord?
Were you there when they crucified my Lord?
Oh! Sometimes it causes me to tremble,
tremble,
tremble.
Were you there when they crucified my Lord?

Contents

Preface

If theology is to have meaning, it must be relevant to human thought, feeling, and experience. This is to say that theology should be relevant to human life. Being relevant means that theology will speak meaningfully and substantively to human conditions. In other words, theology should—indeed must—address the existential realities of people in a pertinent way. Otherwise, it is nothing more than irrelevant intellectual theory.

One reality with which theology must be concerned is that of extreme human suffering. There are times when life is so absurd and extreme that the boundaries of rationality are surpassed and the realm of reasonable explanation is shattered. These are the times when people are thrust into the arena of the inexplicable. They must endure wrenching emotional distress. During these times of emotional catastrophe, mere intellectual inquiry is insufficient. When people reach the sphere of extreme suffering, fundamental questions about God surface. Where is God amid the extremities and absurdities of abject human suffering? This book seeks an answer to that perplexing question.

My interest in probing this question is born out of the convergence of three paths. The first path is that of pastoral ministry. While traveling along this path, I have had the opportunity to observe extreme suffering and the peculiar privilege of walking with people through the "valley of the shadow of death." I refer to this as privilege because, as a pastor, I have been thankful for the opportunity and invitation to minister to people in these moments when ministry is so desperately needed.

The second path is that of culture. As an African American, I am cognizant that my heritage did not originate on American soil. Yet I cannot, nor do I desire to, avoid the reality that I am, in part, a descendent of African and African-American slaves. I feel no need to romanticize my own lineage by insisting that I am necessarily a descendent of royalty. I have no shame in my heritage. What I do have is a craving to discern something of how my suffering matriarchs and patriarchs managed to survive the atrocities of slavery despite the horrendous realities of chattel slavery in North America.

The third path is that of theological reflection. Since I am a Christian, the Bible is an indispensable source for my theological conceptualizations and articulations. For me, the Bible is not ancillary to my own experience. The Bible helps me interpret my experience, and my experience helps me interpret the Bible. I look to Jesus for lessons of faith in Christian Scripture. How did Jesus approach the supreme struggle of surrender to God's will above his own? How did Jesus endure the dreadful tragedy of his crucifixion? How did Jesus overcome his dreadful disaster in the miraculous victory of the resurrection? Lessons learned here are instructive for all who want to be Christian.

My living at the intersection of these three paths has allowed this book to come forth. This text is not offered as an authoritative dictum but as a proposal born out of a definitive faith in God who can do anything—except fail.

Acknowledgments

Numerous people have contributed to this book. For each of them, I am thankful. I am grateful for the confidence and support of Robert Ellsberg and Dwight Hopkins in this project and my abilities. The University of Louisville provided time for research, which facilitated the completion of this effort. Special mention is due my colleagues in the Department of Pan African Studies for the ongoing encouragement and support that made this phase of the journey more joyous.

I am appreciative to those who both challenged and nurtured the development of the precursor to this project—my Ph.D. dissertation at The Southern Baptist Theological Seminary in Louisville, Kentucky. I especially mention William L. Hendricks, Molly Truman Marshall, T. Vaughn Walker, and E. Frank Tupper. Additionally, J. Deotis Roberts and Lewis V. Baldwin opened theological and historical doors that continue to prove priceless.

Finally, First Baptist Church, Eminence, Kentucky, and my father and pastor, W. H. Goatley, Sr., gave me opportunities to learn; First Baptist Church, Campbellsville, Kentucky, where I served as pastor, gave me opportunities to lead. The nurture of my family of origin and the joy of my own immediate family allow me to know the presence of God in ways that make this journey bright.

Introduction

Extreme human suffering raises profound questions about the nature of God. The coexistence of pervasive suffering around the world and belief in a providential God of love is difficult to reconcile. The African-American experience includes historic and contemporary suffering. The life of African Americans invites the difficult question concerning the presence of God in relationship to the suffering of the African diaspora and the majority of the peoples of the world. Historically, black theology has used the experience of black people as a touchstone for theological reflection, and while an integral component of black experience is frequently described as suffering or oppression, this integral component can, at times, be articulated in terms of God-forsakenness.

The inability of many contemporary African Americans to successfully negotiate the complexities of life in the United States is distressing. One would think that African Americans would generally enjoy a greater degree of personal fulfillment, family stability, and economic progress in the post-Civil Rights Movement era. For many, however, this is not so. Consequently, a continuing debate proceeds about the relative advantages and disadvantages that have resulted from the Civil Rights Movement. Nevertheless, while the debate continues, one is prompted to ask why so many contemporary African Americans appear to be spiritually, morally, and materially anemic.

Much of current African-American life can be characterized in terms of human suffering. Why is this so? The equation consists of the long shadow of slavery, segregation, and discrimination to which African Americans have been subjected on North American shores. The equation also includes personal, family, and community responses to the above tragedies. The question remains for the Christian, however, as to where God is in this equation.

What is happening to black America today? Whence the suffering, and what does one have to say about God from within the horrors of abject human suffering? Perhaps there are lessons to be learned from the pain of Christian African-American slaves and the passion of Jesus of Nazareth. An examination of the theology of African-American slaves can make a constructive contribution to the question of where God is amid the experience of Godforsakenness. Further, moving toward an understanding of the Markan narrative surrounding Jesus' cry of forsakenness can move one toward a meaningful response to the question about the presence or absence of God for those whose life circumstances prevent them from experiencing God's presence.

In contrast to the dismay concerning the present dire conditions of much of black America, I am amazed at the degree of survival and occasional thriving of African slaves and their descendants, given the detrimental circumstances with which slaves lived. Further, I have long been fascinated by the cry of dereliction from Jesus, the Son of God, while dying on the cross (Mark 15:34). This study is an attempt to examine these ordeals of anguish and move toward an understanding of where God is during the extremities of human suffering.

During the summer of 1992, I studied in Buenos Aires, Argentina. One dimension of Argentinean life is affluence and prosperity. Buenos Aires is a major cultural and business center in Latin America. However, severe poverty stands in stark contrast to the prosperity of Buenos Aires. Most people have no access to health care, and the quality of care available to the few is minimal. Many poor families live on open land and literally build walls around themselves as they find spare wood, tin, and other materials. Other families must rummage through garbage dumps to salvage usable items from the refuse of the city. While observing these families, elderly people, and children from the window of a bus, I asked myself, with tears in my eyes, "Where is God in all of this?"

The pervasive suffering I witnessed in Buenos Aires is not isolated. Human suffering is encountered around the world, and the question about the presence of God is repeatedly evoked. Famine and tribal warfare in eastern Africa; civil war in Liberia, Somalia, Rwanda, and the former Yugoslavia; human rights violations in Southeast Asia; economic colonialization in Latin America; the hopelessness of blighted rural communities and deserted urban ghettos in the United States; and other innumerable examples of human suffering provoke a question of whether God has forsaken the majority of humanity. Encountering the magnitude of these tragic existences provokes earnest reflection on Jesus' cry of dereliction while he was dying on the cross. "My God, my God, why have you forsaken me?"

The intent of this book is to employ narrative methodology with regard to slave narratives and spirituals and move toward an understanding of the concept of Godforsakenness. After examining Godforsakenness in slave theology, the Markan account of Jesus' crucifixion will be studied, with special attention to the concept of Jesus' Godforsakenness. In light of the extremity of human suffering currently encountered by African Americans, the crisis of Godforsakenness will be considered from within the context of a community that knows all too well what it means to experience the forsakenness of God.

Chapter one will discuss the appropriateness of narrative methodology for African-American theological discourse. The historic role of narrative will be considered, along with the contemporary application of narrative methodology for present theology from African-American perspectives.

Chapter two examines antebellum African-American reflections of slave life to ascertain something of the concept of Godforsakenness in slave thought. Godforsakenness is defined in terms of family separation, physical and psychological violence, sexual exploitation of females, and the anomie that existed in the wake of the dissolution of slavery.

Chapter three articulates the rationale for employing slave-era spirituals to understand theological conceptualizations concerning suffering and the crucifixion of Jesus. Spirituals of this genre are analyzed to determine how antebellum African Americans theologically processed the idea of Godforsakenness.

Chapter four attempts to interpret Jesus' cry of dereliction in Mark's gospel, based on the hermeneutic of antebellum African-American theological concepts of Godforsakenness as found in their spirituals. Mark's narrative treatment of the relationship of Jesus and his disciples is employed paradigmatically as pointing toward Jesus' experience of his relationship with God at the crucifixion.

Chapter five endeavors to articulate the relevance of the conclusions drawn for theology today. It offers a constructive proposal for articulating an interpretation of Godforsakenness and suggests the applicability for contemporary contextual constructive theologies.

CHAPTER ONE

Narrative and African-American Theology

Due to the nature of theology and the culture of African peoples, narrative is essential to African-American theology. In classical African-American form, theology is revelational and biblical. Narrative is integral to it because the use of story is firmly established in the history of African cultures. In this chapter, we will consider historical and theological grounds for African-American narrative theology.

HISTORY AND NARRATIVE

Black Americans have a rich history of oral communication that reaches back to their African roots. African literature included tales, proverbs, and riddles that were transmitted from generation to generation by amateur storytellers or cultural narrators—*griots*. When Africans were uprooted from their homes and brought to the New World as slaves, their oral tradition was preserved. This tradition contributed to the continuity of aspects of African thought and life, despite the atrocities of chattel slavery.

Narrative and African Society

African civilizations rose and fell centuries before Europeans sailed along Africa's coasts on exploitative voyages to India. Highly sophisticated societies transmitted religious and cultural value systems and philosophical ideas through generations by means of "artistically complex oral narrative performances, rather than by written word."[1] Michelle Cliff explains:

1

When the slave traders descended on the west coast of Africa in the sixteenth century and thereafter (the Atlantic slave trade lasted from about 1550 to 1850), they were met by inhabitants of urbanized, advanced, and sophisticated civilizations. Of all the nation/groups [such as the Yoruba, the Kongo, the Fon, the Ewe, the Mande, and the Ejagham], only the Ejagham were or could be considered a rural people, and they had organized towns as well as rural settlements. All the other nation/groups were highly and complexly urbanized, and had been urbanized since what Europeans call the Dark Ages.[2]

African society used narrative to socialize the young. The most effective way to implement this method of socialization was to tell theologically significant stories. African societies assumed a functional intent for theology, and no child could be considered prepared for life without being firmly grounded in the oral tradition. This doctrine-in-narrative form was functional, not apologetic. It could use familiar people and animals as symbols without fear of challenges to the symbols' intellectual respectability. The intent was exclusively to improve the quality of life. Tales were told for their value to the common life, so their interpretation involved no need for scientific historical verification.[3]

The significance of narrative in the life of African people survived the torturous passages from the coasts of Africa to the shores of the New World. In this new and tragic environment, narrative served as an important element of the slave communities that the Africans would now constitute.

Narrative and Slave Communities

One sign of African influence on African-American slave culture was the place of tales in the life of the slave community. They were to a large degree pedagogical, making the past part of the present. Tales primarily functioned to service contemporary needs, while songs and sermons tended to service historical needs.

Tales functioned significantly in slave communities, teaching morality and survival skills. They taught people how to conduct their lives. Stories were told that explained the fate of those who forgot their dependency on God. Others taught the value of everyday human relationships. Family relationships, values, and obligations were prominent themes, as well as courtship and marriage. Slave tales addressed a range of issues that were important to understand, if one was to survive the horrors of chattel slavery.

> [Slave tales] were utilized to inculcate a vision of the good and moral life by stressing the ideals of friendship, cooperation, meaningful activity, and family love. . . . The situation of the slave and freedman made survival a paramount concern, and it is not surprising that this need gave a practical cast to much of their folklore. . . . It was dangerous for black men and women to forget who or where they were, and this danger constituted a motif running through Negro tales.[4]

Little fantasy or romanticism is found in slave tales. The plight of the slaves was so imperiled that they could not indulge themselves, so tales focused on proper conduct and righteous living. The tales also taught strategies for survival. These survival techniques are best known through animal trickster tales, which were "of all the narratives of social protest or psychological release, among the easiest to relate both within and especially outside the group."[5]

The trickster tales were obsessed with the weak manipulating the strong, reversing the structures of power. The fundamental element of the trickster tales was how the weak used their wits to evade the strong. "The characteristic spirit of these tales was one not of moral judgment but of vicarious triumph."[6] Trickster tales were particularly used to redefine the realities of life in bondage. Further, the tales taught slaves how to negotiate the complex matrix of relationships and structure of slavery. Additionally, tales served to enhance the self-image of slaves and created a sense of community, yielding a cohesive identity.[7] Beyond the tales of slaves, the story of the Bible was a significant part of the experience of many.

Slaves were generally forbidden to read and write, but they developed creative symbolisms communicated through their orality. Consequently, slaves were introduced to the Bible by white preachers. Some white preachers of the Great Evangelical Awakenings may have been genuinely interested in the conversion of the slaves to North Atlantic Christianity. Most of these plantation preachers, however, misused the

Bible to encourage docility and submission to the slaveholding community.[8]

Nevertheless, slaves reinterpreted their "religious" instruction. As slaves became more familiar with the Bible, they appropriated it, primarily through storytelling. The black preacher became the dominant storyteller and told the stories of God's liberating activity in the lives of God's suffering people. Slaves found commonality in their suffering and that of God's people—Israel. Thus liberation became a dominant theme of their Bible stories.

THEOLOGY AND NARRATIVE

African-American theology in its classical sense is necessarily biblical theology and therefore presumed to be revelational. While some may not interpret all scripture literally, the contention that the Bible is the revealed, inspired Word of God compels one to take all scripture seriously. I emphasize *classical* African-American theology in the sense that this type of theology is time-honored, well-established, archetypal theology vis-à-vis perspectives that are essentially reductions of theology to cultural critique. While theology inherently brings a multifaceted critique to human social intercourse and tradition, to engage in social analysis from an alleged place of privilege under the guise of theology is, at best, inappropriate and, at worst, blasphemous. The exemplar African-American theological perspective with which I am concerned is biblical and revelational.

Hermeneutics

Because classical African-American theology is biblical and revelational, in its best sense, it employs a socio-critical rather than socio-pragmatic hermeneutic theory. These two ways of understanding can be differentiated as follows. Socio-pragmatic hermeneutics analyzes, interprets, and proposes conclusions exclusively from within the social mores of a given contextual community. On the other hand, socio-critical hermeneutics seeks to use dimensions that are not bound within a particular contextual horizon, and therefore, functions as a liberating critique which frees one from oppressive and manipulative interpretations and applications.[9]

To argue that socio-critical hermeneutics is preferable to socio-pragmatic hermeneutics is not to deny the positive contributions that philosophical pragmatism offers the theological task. One could effectively argue that this approach makes a positive contribution, inasmuch as the nature or acquired norms of a given community provide the evaluative parameters that have traditionally been ascribed to rationality and argument (yet the latter are not thereby excluded). This perspective guards against proponents of one particular worldview dictating the terms of rationality and argumentation to proponents of other worldviews. Some Eurocentric approaches to theological hermeneutics that have dominated Western scholarship have been severely criticized by Christians who recognize the inadequacies of Eurocentric approaches for Two-Thirds World cultures[10] and minority cultures oppressed in the West.[11] The thought of Cornel West, for example, convincingly follows a rigorous path of Afro-American critical thought that is rooted in prophetic Christian thought and American pragmatism.[12]

West contends that in spite of its limitations, "pragmatism provides an American context for Afro-American thought, a context that imparts to it both a shape and a heritage of philosophical legitimacy."[13] Furthermore, West argues that articulating Afro-American religious philosophy requires sophisticated skills of interpretation and description, imagination and reflection, logic and analysis. "This is not a geographical or existential removal, but an intellectual one which acknowledges the demands of the discipline [of religious philosophy]."[14]

The principal problematic aspect of an obdurate proposal for Afro-American pragmatic thought, however, is its delimitation to the problems of race and class encountered by Afro-Americans in the northern hemisphere. West calls attention to how Josiah Royce, William James, George Santayana, and John Dewey[15] remained unaffected by brutalities inflicted upon Afro-Americans. However, while pragmatism moves toward freedom for Afro-Americans, it may fail to adequately relate this concern for freedom with the struggle for liberation by women of color and the oppressed in non-African contexts. Those who are oppressed in various Two-Thirds World countries, as well as the unraveling eastern European countries, face oppressive opposition from related economic and political powers, as do Afro-Americans. Afro-Americans cannot attain freedom without the corresponding liberation of Latin Americans, Asians, oppressed eastern Europeans, and the like. Afro-Americans cannot be free until all are free. Consequently, socio-pragmatism is not the most useful hermeneutic for African-American theology.

Socio-critical hermeneutics, however, penetrates beneath the surface functions of texts, traditions, and institutions to expose their roles of power, domination, or manipulation.[16] This approach is necessary in theology because certain ways of biblical reading in Western traditions clearly have served to affirm, support, or enforce various prejudices and forms of oppression.[17] Cain Hope Felder suggests that the theological community is challenged to search for modes of hermeneutics more relevant to blacks and other Two-Thirds World peoples. Theology cannot be allowed to remain constrained within the historic socioreligious context of the Greco-Roman world or contemporary Eurocentrism. Felder observes:

> Of all the mandates confronting the Church today, the mandate of the world community predicated on a renewed commitment to pluralism and the attendant acknowledgment of the integrity of all racial groups constitutes an urgent agenda for Bible scholars and laity alike.[18]

Socio-critical hermeneutics serves to rescue texts from Western hegemony, thereby rediscovering truth and leading toward the liberation of both people and biblical texts. Considering the dimensions of the existential reality of the life-world and the trans- contextual critique of systems, socio-critical hermeneutics strives to expose abusive manipulations, rediscover truth, and oppose self-deceptions that function in texts.[19]

To this end, an approach like that of J. Deotis Roberts' proposal of existential ontology holds promise for African-American theology. Existential ontology is subjective and objective. It is introspective and addresses reality. Existential ontology is concerned with freedom, but it is painfully aware of and actively engaged with the larger reality of racism. However, the subjective-objective character of existential ontology is not perfectly symmetrical. Roberts' inclination is more toward the practical than toward pure reason. This he attributes to the philosophical predisposition of black reflection on experience that is related to insight or intuition.

The philosophy of the Black experience is a type of knowledge. It is like *prajna* or non-knowing knowledge. That is to say, it is not rational knowledge, but insightful knowledge. It is knowing from the inside rather than from the outside. It is characteristic of Blacks that they have learned about life from living it. Knowledge of experience more than book knowledge has been the basis of the Black experience. And as we have observed, even the intellectual Black man eventually finds his greatest philosophy at the point where thought touches life. We had to learn about life by living rather than thinking about living. Thus our reflection is based upon the realities of our existence. It is ontological-existential reflection.[20]

Existential ontology is an appropriate proposal for a black socio-critical hermeneutic theory. This theory is neither purely subjective nor objective. It passes the test of attending to the dynamic axiological tension between both system and life-world. Existential ontology is not a socio-pragmatic theory, because it does not isolate itself from external critique. Instead, it invites scrutiny from within and without and stands as a true approach to hermeneutics that seeks to "develop an *emancipatory critique* in hermeneutics which reaches beyond the horizons of particular persons or communities."[21]

Socio-critical hermeneutics and narrative methodology are inherently compatible tools with which to engage the African-American theology task. Just as socio-critical hermeneutics extends beyond the limitations of one's contextual horizons, story belongs to all people. Stories convey both systemic concepts and particular characteristics. They allow people within communities to communicate and permit communication between different communities. Narrative is an appropriate methodology to facilitate understanding within the African-American socio-critical hermeneutic theory of existential ontology.

The classical African-American Christian theological perspective that seeks a genuinely liberating approach to biblical texts presupposes the centrality of the Bible. This bibliocentric viewpoint is born from the conviction that the Bible is the story of God's revelation from creation to consummation. The biblical story, however, is not the only story essential to African-American theology. The biblical story is understood in relationship to the African-American story. Further, the interplay of these two stories is communicated through oral and imaginative telling of the stories.

Orality and Imagination

Renita J. Weems argues that the significance of orality in African-American narrative can be attributed to the history of the early exposure of the Bible to black people. Slaves were first exposed to the Bible through public reading or sermons; they were not permitted to read or write. Weems implies that the importance of orality in African-American narrative is related to this historical context, as well as to the reality that black North Americans have only been allowed to read in large numbers for little more than a century.[22] The oral character of African-American narrative of which Weems speaks is not an exercise of recitation by rote. Instead, African-American narrative has an inherent imaginative quality.

J. Deotis Roberts describes the black religious experience as principally an oral tradition that is more intuitive than conceptual. Therefore, black theology needs a method primarily based upon image-thinking, which is a large part of the black experience. Religion is a cohesive aspect of black culture. "The arts, poetry, music, and the like, are closely associated with religion."[23] Thus imagination plays a decisive role in African-American aesthetics, literature, music, and theology.

Vincent L. Wimbush explains that African slaves employed a hermeneutic with qualities of "looseness" and "playfulness" that is reflected in songs, sermons, addresses, and exhortations vis-à-vis biblical texts.

The interpretation was not controlled by the literal words of the texts, but by social experience. The texts were heard more than read; they were engaged as stories that seized and freed the imagination. Interpretation was therefore controlled by the freeing of the collective consciousness and imagination of the African slaves as they heard the biblical stories and retold them to reflect their actual social situation, as well as their visions for something different. Many of the biblical stories, themselves the product of cultures with well-established oral traditions, functioned sometimes as allegory, as parable, or as veiled social criticism. Such stories well served the African slaves, not only on account of their well-established oral traditions, but also because their situation dictated veiled or indirect social criticism—"hitting a straight lick with a crooked stick."[24]

The narrative quality of scripture requires the use of imagination.[25] Historical-critical studies are enriched by imaginative reading that enables one to relate the present to the text of the scripture. Black preachers without formal theological education have long used imagination in their preaching. They would sometimes say, "In my mind of imagination, I can see . . . ," or "Let me use my sanctified imagination." Imagination sees the symbolism of texts and "opens the text toward the transformation of the person and society."[26]

Thomas Hoyt, Jr., suggests three principle reasons for using imagination in biblical interpretation. First, imaginative reading allows scripture to be read as it is intended to be read. Scripture is not raw material for theological or ethical systematic formulation. It is "for formation of the church, in order that the society might be transformed." Second, imaginative reading allows everyone access to scripture rather than only an elite group of specialists. Third, in imaginative reading "the evocative power of these images, coupled with the sociological grid of the reader, leads to new and exciting meanings and ideas." The result is that scripture can have a myriad of meanings. "Sensitivity to images means that we must allow other persons to express their interpretations, which may indeed be of profit to us."[27] Thus imagination is integral to narrative methodology, and narrative methodology is essential for African-American theology. Furthermore, just as narrative is integral to African-American theology, it is likewise foundational from an African-American historical perspective.

SUMMARY

Contemporary African-American theology takes seriously the experience of black people. The dominant influence upon the religious development of Africans and black North Americans has been the struggle for meaningful existence.[28] Suffering is a transcendent cultural reality encountered by black people and experienced in two ways. First, black people share suffering that is common to all of humanity—illness, broken relationships, death, accidents, wars, and the like.

Second, black suffering has been experienced because of slavery, discrimination, and racism. "This sociological grid of blacks provides a solidarity that transcends even membership in the Christian religion."[29]

The people's experiences are found in their stories—their narratives—and narrative is woven throughout the tapestry of the lives of Africans and the African diaspora. Narrative's contemporary significance therefore springs forth from the historical and theological contexts of African culture. Consequently, narrative method is apropos for African-American theology.

Narrative was a critical component of the history of African and African-American people, and narrative methodology is a crucial element for African-American theological reflection and discourse. Further, while tales are an example of how important stories were in African-American life, one's own life stories were, and are, imperative vehicles for communicating the experiences of one's own life and the core of one's own faith. "Only narrative form," says Stephen Crites, "can contain the tensions, the surprises, the disappointments and reversals and achievements of actual, temporal experience."[30] We now turn to the narratives of former slaves to hear the stories of their encounters with the extremities of human suffering.

CHAPTER TWO

Antebellum African-American Godforsakenness

Understanding a people entails listening to their stories. Historical, archaeological, and sociological research, as well as other disciplines, are critical for grasping essential contextual considerations when studying communities, but stories communicate the essence of a people's identity.[1] This chapter will discuss the Godforsakenness of North American slavery in a general context. Then it will examine the Godforsakenness of slavery, primarily through narratives of former slaves and, to a lesser degree, through observations of some involved in missionary efforts to former slaves. These narratives discuss the suffering of slaves in terms of family separations, the victimization of violence, the particularity of female sexual exploitation, and the anomie that ensued in the wake of slavery's dissolution.[2] As these narratives are presented, the reader should be able to experience something of the Godforsakenness known to slaves.

Where is God when people are confronted with prolonged agonizing suffering? Is God present yet intentionally silent, ineffective, or impotent? Is God absent? These questions are different from questions related to theodicy, which has to do with justifying the existence of a good and omnipotent God in the face of undeserved suffering or evil. This book will not explicitly address issues related to God's power and righteousness in the face of wickedness. The present concern is to reflect on the issue of whether God is present with those who endure the extremities of human suffering—in this case African and African-American slaves.[3]

The above-mentioned experiences of suffering are identified in this study as Godforsakenness. In the context of this study, God-forsakenness calls for certain a priori conditions. First there must be a concept of the immanence of a personal God. Transcendence can be characteristic, but the personal character of God is assumed. God must be conceived of, at least in part, as personal, present, and involved. Next, one must be able to experience God. God must be able to be known and encountered in order that immanence can be conceived. Implied here is the notion of the goodness of God as a recognizable attribute.

Given these two conditions, one can know Godforsakenness when the positive experiences of life—both actual and conceptual—which are in some measure attributable to the goodness of the immanent God, are radically reversed, transforming life into an abyss of negativity and destruction. Well-formed life becomes deformed. Humanity is consumed by inhumanity. This radical reversal of a life of freedom, community, well-being, sexual integrity, and modest order (at least according to the conventions of a given era) becomes enslavement, broken family bonds, sexual exploitation, and anomie. Although antebellum African Americans may not have employed the term *Godforsakenness* in their vernacular, one could accurately call this radical reversal Godforsakenness, since the horrific circumstances of slavery appear to correspond with the extremities associated with the concept of Godforsakenness.

It is conceded that all human suffering is not Godforsakenness and all Godforsakenness is not located in the context of African-American slavery. Godforsakenness theoretically represents the extremities of human suffering. Nevertheless, human suffering that is not Godforsakenness is no less legitimate suffering. Further, extreme human suffering points toward the experience of Godforsakenness. Through the narratives that follow, we will attempt to discern something of the slaves' experience of Godforsakenness.

THE GODFORSAKENNESS OF NORTH AMERICAN SLAVERY

When one is confronted with evil, the critical issue has nothing to do with metaphysical speculation. The issue is the internal crises related to humanity's historical reality and existential encounters with wickedness, sin, disaster, and the like. According to Chaim Potok, "The presence of evil, its reality, makes a hole in the heart of the believer."[4]

Traditional theological and philosophical approaches to God and evil address contradictions related to God's omnipotence, God's goodness, and evil's existence, all of which cannot logically stand together. Any combination of two necessarily eliminates the third. Harold M. Schulweis insightfully identifies the problematic approaches of theologians and philosophers of religion who separate the problem of evil from the integral context of personal faith. Schulweis's argument holds that theologians' and philosophers' examinations of the problem of evil apart from an integral connection with the holistic character of monotheistic faith results in "the dissatisfaction of the believer with their solutions."[5]

The Self-Revelation of God

Christian theology presupposes God's self-revelation. God is not known through human discovery; God is mystery. Augustine followed earlier Greek theologians: "*Si comprehendis, non est Deus* (If you have understood, then what you have understood is not God)."[6] God is known by divine disclosure. Karl Barth succinctly explains that Jesus Christ "is the history of God with man [sic] and the history of man with God."[7] Yet humanity's understanding of God's being through God's self-disclosure is provisional.[8] Hence one logically, and sometimes painfully, inquires as to the nature of God who reveals Godself.

In classical theology, God is perceived as, among other things, transcendent yet immanent, just yet merciful, strong yet compassionate. Further, God is traditionally considered loving and faithful. However, if one accepts the premise that God is generally loving and faithful to creation and particularly to those who love God, one faces a critical dilemma of attempting to hold in tension the dichotomy of a loving and faithful God and the inexplicable horror that has and does terrorize, humiliate, and dehumanize individuals and communities.

The General Nature of Chattel Slavery

Slavery has been part of various cultures throughout human history, but the fundamental nature of slavery has varied in kind and intensity. Slavery has not usually been based on race. Instead, slavery has been employed with diverse rationales and varying degrees of servitude. Some have become slaves through imprisonment from war. People have entered slavery as a necessary solution to economic indebtedness. Slavery has been employed as a strategy for people in lower economic statuses to gain higher status through servitude to wealthier people. Further, slavery has been used by communities whose social orders have been organized around the concept of kinspeople to contend with foreigners without kinspeople in the community. Slavery in the New World, however, was distinctive in that the majority of the slaves in the Americas were Africans. Unlike slavery in other cultures throughout human history, North American slavery was almost exclusively grounded on the basis of racial identity.[9]

The experiences of African slave immigrants were radically different from the experiences of European immigrants. European immigrants normally brought with them their customs, foods, and other cultural distinctives, which contributed positively to the continuation and propagation of their cultural identities. The racial foundation of American slavery, however, sought to deny Africans the opportunity to retain their cultural practices and identities.

> Overnight [captured Africans] were transformed from merchants, or Arabic scholars, or craftsmen, or peasant farmers, or cattle-tenders to American slaves. They ate what they were given, not what they wanted. They dressed in the clothes that were given them, not those they had known in the past. African women were . . . made commodities, unprotected by a traditional morality, without specific places and functions, sexually exploited by the master and even deprived of a full relationship with their children.[10]

African slaves faced efforts of deculturalization intended to indoctrinate them in a new way of life. Africans faced demands to relinquish their ways of life. Some succumbed and others resisted.

The pressure on Africans to conform to something different from that to which they were accustomed began during the Middle Passage—the voyage from Africa to the Americas. This voyage could accurately be described as a veritable nightmare. "There was hardly standing, lying, or sitting room" aboard the ships that carried the slaves to the shores of their new homes. "Chained together by twos, hands and feet, the slaves had no room in which to move about and no freedom to exercise their bodies even in the slightest. . . ."[11] Ships were overcrowded, and the overcrowding contributed to incidents and epidemics of disease from which few slaves escaped. A diary entry of a slave trader in 1800 indicates the horror of slaves during the Middle Passage:

> Blacks rebellious. Crew uneasy. Our linguist says their mourning is a prayer for death, ours and their own. Some try to starve themselves. Lost three this morning. Leaped with crazy laughter to the waiting sharks, sang as they went under. . . . [12]

African slaves were subjected to dehumanizing experiences and environments intended to strip them of their sense of community and culture.

The longer Africans lived on American shores, the more the stringent rules the slaveholders developed to assure control of the slaves' lives in every conceivable way. During the late eighteenth and early nineteenth centuries, Black Codes were developed in the South for the purpose of regulating all aspects of slave life. These repressive regulatory statutes were devised within an ideological construct that held that slaves were property and the rights of white slaveholders were to be protected. John Hope Franklin explains:

> A slave could not strike a white person, even in self-defense; but the killing of a slave however malicious, was rarely regarded as murder. The rape of a female slave was regarded as a crime only because it involved trespassing on and destroying the property of another person.[13]

Every segment of the slaves' lives was restricted. Slaves could not own property, buy and sell goods, visit the homes of whites or free blacks, assemble without a white person present, or handle literature considered incendiary by whites. The restrictions on slaves' lives were enforced by patrols of free white men who would apprehend blacks without appropriate documentation and return them to their slaveholders or place them in prison. At other times, patrols would harass and victimize slaves at will.

Slavery in the Americas was fundamentally a racist institution. Constant pressure was applied on the slaves, with the intent that they would lose their cultural identities. Every aspect of their lives was regulated. These are consistent characteristics of life in North American slavery. However, there was no uniform response to slavery by the enslaved. "We must conceive of the slave personality as an ambivalent one. On the one hand are submissiveness and a sense that one deserves to be a slave," says George P. Rawick, "on the other is a great deal of anger in the ways that protect the personality and have objective results in the improvement of the slaves' situation and eventual liberation, at least from chattel slavery."[14]

To assert that slaves were either infantile or radical revolutionaries is erroneous. Slaves responded to exploitation and oppression in various ways. Some slaves became docile "Sambos" while others rose up and rebelled in the tradition of Nat Turner, Denmark Vessey, and Gabriel Prosser.[15]

Slaveholding Christians and their sympathizers developed an anthropology to justify chattel slavery in a professed Christian culture. Riggins R. Earl, Jr., notes two theological responses to the question of the anthropology of slaves—the naturalist response and the Christian master response.[16] Pro-slavery literature is replete with the naturalist assumption of the irrelevance of posing questions of whether slaves' theological anthropology was *imago Dei*. Naturalists assigned slaves the subhuman classification of primates. This classification was necessitated because of the alleged phenomenological observations of the primitive and uncivilized character of Africans on their own continent. Consequently, mental and spiritual oppression existed concurrently with physical subjugation. Additionally, the physical darkness of slaves was interpreted to indicate their anthropological inferiority in relation to the white slaveholding population.

Christian slaveholders constructed a theological anthropology that gave theological respectability to slavery. This Christian master approach propagated a dualism of soul and body, which allowed slaveholders to rationalize the respectability of chattel slavery. By conceptually separating the body and soul of slaves in this construct, slaveholders justified abusive behavior to slaves' bodies while simultaneously contending that only slaves' souls had intrinsic value. Earl argues that the Christian master approach was also necessary for a theological rebuttal to the challenges of northern abolitionist Christians and theologians.[17]

Apologists for slavery failed to address adequately the atrocities committed against those held in slavery. Apologists would argue that slavery benefitted African "savages" or "pagans" by bringing them to a Christian land; slave life in the New World provided exposure to civility for Africans unknown in their own lands; and similar "privileges" and "benefits" of slavery for the enslaved. However, slavery is described by historian T. J. Morgan as "a monster, and the mother of vices."[18] Carter J. Jackson summarizes the experience of slavery of untold millions of African slaves and their descendants when he states, "If you's wants to know 'bout slavery time, it was Hell."[19] It is to accounts of experiences of this "Hell" of slavery to which we now turn. We will listen to stories of the Godforsakenness of slave life as expressed through experiences of the separation of families, violence, women's exploitation, and anomie following manumission.

While slaves had varying responses to the exploitation and oppression of chattel slavery, slave narratives clearly communicate the fact that the overwhelming majority of slaves faced these traumatic realities. Even those who claim not to have been personally subjected to the dehumanizing viciousness of the slaveholding community testify to witnessing brutality directed against other slaves.

In these stories, one is provoked to one of many possible responses. One may experience rage and anger toward individuals and the system responsibile for perpetuating the atrocities of slavery. One may respond in absolute denial—the atrocities reported could not actually be inflicted on humans by other humans. One may respond with intense grief and sympathy. One may be provoked to inquire as to the presence or absence of God in the lives of those whose stories relate inexplicable accounts of separation, violence, exploitation, and confusion.

THE GODFORSAKENNESS OF FAMILY SEPARATIONS

Community was an integral part of African culture; abandonment and loneliness were encountered when slaves experienced loss of community. The importance of community was essential to Africans before their encounter with Americans. Following the capture of Africans, individuals from various cultural groups were forced into ships bound for North America, and community began to develop under adverse conditions. Rather than building community because of common ancestry and perhaps common economic good, Yorubas, Akans, Ibos, Angolans, and others began developing community on slave ships, where common horrors of frightful shrieks, human stench, and turbulent seas were shared. According to Sterling Stuckey, "slave ships were the first real incubators of slave unity across cultural lines, cruelly revealing irreducible links from one ethnic group to the other. . . ."[20]

When slaves were taken from Africa, their relationships to their primary social units—family, village, and clan—were severed. This dramatically challenged the psyche of African people who lived with the consciousness that "a man is a man through other men [sic]." Communal consciousness evolved as an integral dimension of life in slave quarters.

> The tendency of quarter people to view themselves as a familial group, with a common life-style, common interests and problems, and a common need to stick together is a theme which appears frequently in the black source material. Whatever their personal jealousies and animosities, as a group the members of the quarter community identified each other as a distinct body of persons tied together by a common historical experience, by a common philosophical and behavioral approach to the world, and by their common struggles against the pressures and demands of slavery.[21]

The sense of community is further illustrated in the folktale "How the Slaves Helped Each Other."[22] Simon Brown tells how the slaves cared for one another during illness.

> In slavery time, Simon explained, only white folks had doctors or nurses to care for them. Still, if a slave became ill, he wasn't left alone to suffer unattended. In time of illness or other trouble, fellow slaves would "turn in and help out."[23]

Community was essential to the identity and survival of slaves. It was a natural development of a people confronted with the common horrors of living with the irrational duality of slavery. Slaveholders contended that slaves were essentially subhuman but strove to convert them to a religion that stressed humanity and divinity.[24] Slaveholders treated slaves as children but expected them to conduct themselves with sufficient maturity and responsibility to support the farms and families of the slaveholders. Whites looked on blacks as barbarians, yet were fascinated by their songs, dances, and tales. The irrationality of institutional slavery meant that strong communal bonds were never safe from disruption.

> The life of every slave could be altered by the most arbitrary and amoral acts. They could be whipped, sexually assaulted, ripped out of societies in which they had deep roots, and bartered away for pecuniary profit by men and women who were also capable of treating them with kindness and consideration and who professed belief in a moral code which they held up for emulation not only by their children but often by their slaves as well.[25]

Runaway Slaves

The fragile slave community was particularly threatened when slaves ran away or were sold. Certain slaves found that remaining a slave was no longer bearable. Frederick Douglass reasoned, "I have only one life to lose. I had as well be killed running as die standing."[26] Stephen Pembroke described the condition of slavery as "a hard substance; you cannot break it nor pull it apart, and the only way is to escape from it."[27]

When slaves decided that it was necessary to flee, there remained the pain of losing important relationships. In an 1846 speech, Lewis Richardson described the cost of escape. "I can truly say that I have only one thing to lament over, and that is my bereft wife, who is yet in bondage."[28] In a letter to one of his former slaveholders, Henry Bibb wrote, "I wish to be remembered in love to my aged mother, and friends; please tell her that if we should never meet again in this life, my prayer shall be to God that we may meet in Heaven, where parting shall be no more."[29]

Family life was radically different in the slave quarters vis-à-vis the slaveholding communities. White family life was cultivated on the basis of the conventions of society and customs. Slave family life was restricted by the convictions (or lack thereof) of particular slaveholders concerning the family. Slaveholders sometimes encouraged monogamous family relationships because of convictions about the importance of family, but most frequently the rationale was related to the control one could exercise over slaves through threats toward slave family members.[30]

The Selling of Slaves

Communal bonds were also severed when family members were sold. Although slaveholders did not separate the majority of slave couples, a callousness is evident in the slaveholders' heartless treatment of couples that were separated.

> The heartlessness of the planters is revealed more clearly in their separation of slaves who had lived together for decades. . . . Hosea Bidell was separated from his mate of twenty-five years; Valentine Miner from his after thirty years; and in the most horrifying case of them all, Lucy Robinson was separated from her mate after living with him for forty-three years.[31]

The fragility of matrimonial bonds was so apparent, according to Susan Hamilton, "One t'ing, no minister nebber say in readin' de matrimony 'let no man put asunder' 'cause a couple would be married tonight an' tomorrow one would be taken away en be sold."[32]

Despite the challenges to strong familial bonds imposed on black families by slavery, family relationships were important. In order for slave men and women to visit each other when they lived in separate places, they would have to secure passes or permits to avoid the risk of being beaten by patrollers. This created a peculiar challenge for husbands and wives who wanted to be together but whose interaction was severely curtailed by the slaveholders. Julia Woodberry remembers:

> You see, de nigger men would want to go to see dey wives en dey would have to get a 'mit [permit] from dey Massa to visit dem. Cose dey wouldn' live together cause dey wives would be here, dere en yonder. It been like dis, sometimes de white folks would sell de wife of one of dey niggers way from dey husband en den another time, dey would sell de husband way from dey wife.[33]

Some slaves risked physical danger in order to spend time with their loved ones who lived on different plantations. These living arrangements were sometimes by force, yet at other times male slaves preferred to live on farms away from their wives to avoid witnessing the exploitation and brutality to which the women would be subjected while the men were helpless to defend their honor. Samuel Boulware's father lived on a plantation two miles away from Boulware's mother. However,

> He would git a pass to come to see mammy once every week. If he come more than dat he would have to skeedaddle through de woods and fields from the patrollers. If they ketched him widout a pass, he was sho' in for a skin crackin' whippin'. He knowed all dat but he would slip to see mammy anyhow, whippin' or not.[34]

One could argue that perhaps the most brutal aspect of slavery was the separation of families. The slave narratives give substantial attention and weight to this experience. Slaves faced the trauma of losing loved ones because they were often valued exclusively in economic terms by slaveholders. Bill Simms said of his master,

> if he got hard up for money, he would advertise and sell some slaves, like my oldest sister was sold on the block with her children. She sold for eleven hundred dollars, a baby in her arms sold for three hundred dollars.[35]

Luke Dixon's grandmother told him how the slave traders would catch people in Africa in order to take them to the New World for a life of chattel slavery.

> They herded them up like cattle and put them in stalls and brought them on the ship and sold them. [Grandma] said some they captured and left bound till they came back and sometimes they never went back to get them. They died. They had room in the stalls on the boat to set down or lie down. They put several together. Put the men to themselves and the women to themselves. When they sold Grandma and Grandpa at a fishing dock called Newport, Va., they had their feet bound down and their hands bound crossed, upon a platform. They sold Grandma's daughter to somebody in Texas. She cried and begged to let them be together. They didn't pay no tension to her. She couldn't talk but she made them know she didn't want to be parted.[36]

Selling members of slave families was an effective disciplinary tool, but family separations were not only exercised for disciplinary reasons. Often the separation of family members had to do with the alleged moral fiber of slaveholders. J. W. C. Pennington recalls a case in which his slaveholder once owned a beautiful twenty-four-year-old woman. One year after her purchase, one of the slaveholder's sons "became attached to her, for no honorable purposes. . . ." Consequently, she was sold to a Georgia slaveholder in front of her weeping parents. The transaction was conducted by the son who violated her while the woman's father, "a pious member and exhorter in the Methodist church," pleaded with the master for time to arrange for someone nearby to purchase his daughter. The slaveholder replied, "She has offended my family, and I can only restore confidence in my family by sending her out of hearing."[37]

While in most cultures healthy, strong children are normally thought of as joys and assets to family life, healthy children born to slaves could become part of the parents' greatest encounters with sorrow and pain. Good health was twisted into a liability for slave families. Will Glass' grandfather explained to him that "when a child was born if it was a child that was fine blooded they would put it on the block and sell it away from its parents while it was little." This happened to both of Glass' grandparents, who never knew their biological parents.[38]

Boulware comments that his slaveholder bought and sold slaves as any other commodity, and no evidence existed to indicate that slave-holders and slave traders considered the humanity of the slaves or the bonds between parents and children. Says Boulware,

It was sad times to see mother and chillun separated. I's seen de slave speculator cut de little nigger chillun with keen leather whips, 'cause they'd cry and run after de wagon dat was takin' their mammies away after they was sold.[39]

Gordon Bluford witnessed the inhumanity encountered by slave parents and children. He saw many slaves sold on the auction block with infants being taken from mothers' arms and mothers and children being sold to separate slave traders. "I saw families separated from each other, some going to one white master and some to another."[40] The viciousness of family separations was exacerbated by the abusive treatment of babies, resulting in their abandonment. Anne Rice remembers that, "Sometimes they would take crowds of slaves to Mississippi, taking away mothers from their infant babies, leaving the babies on the floor."[41]

Tom Douglas describes classically how entire families could be sold and separated. One family, consisting of a man who was a blacksmith, a woman cook, and their child who was a "waitin' boy," were sold. "They wuz put on de block an sold an a diffunt man bought each one an they went ter diffunt part of de country ter live an nevah did see one nother no moah. They wuz sole jes like cows an horses."

Douglas then assesses slavery from his experience and insight by declaring to his interviewer, "No'm, ah didn't like slavery days. Ah'd rather be free an hungry."[42]

Slaves saw their encounters with the horrors of family separations in terms of evil, with slaveholders and slave traders personifying evil. Cureton Milling said of his slaveholder, who broke families through the selling of slaves, "Sometime I think he was de very old Nick turned loose in de earth for a season."[43]

The selling of slaves not only created a sense of insecurity, abandonment, and the personification of evil, it was dehumanizing and humiliating. Slave traders added humiliating insult to the traumatic experience of the slaves by the way in which slaves were sold. The psychological impact of being treated like animals was devastating. If a slave desired to turn to the slave's history for vindication of character, where could one turn? There would be no record of the person as a man or woman. Examination of the records of the slaveholder, even the "old, kind, Christian master," would only reveal one's being catalogued along with farm animals and equipment. Pennington concludes: "However humiliating and degrading it may be to his feelings to find his name written down among the beasts of the field, *that* is just the place, and the *only* place assigned to it by the chattel relation."[44]

Julia Grace tells that after slaves were placed on the trading block and stripped of their clothing, "The man bid 'em off like you'd bid off oxen. They weighed 'em and stripped 'em naked to see if they was anything wrong with 'em and how they was built and then bid 'em off."[45]

Richard Farley's father and mother were "auctioned off just like you would sell goods. One would holler one price and another would holler another, and the highest bid would get the slave."[46] Slaves were denigrated by being treated as if they were animals. "Just stand em up on a block bout three feet high en a speculator bid em off just like dey was horses. . . . I see em sell some slaves twice fore I was sold en I see de slaves when dey be travelin like hogs. . . ."[47]

The breaking up of families was even traumatic for slaves who were too young to comprehend the significance of all that was occurring at the time. The separation of family members left indelible impressions in the minds and hearts of young slave children. William Hamilton was too young to remember the details of being separated from his mother, but he reports, "De only thing I 'members 'bout all dat, am dere am lots of cryin' when dey tooks me 'way from my mammy. Dat something I never forgits."[48]

M. Fowler offers a precise summary of how slaves were victimized by violence against the family. But this victimization of family life was not the extent of the Godforsakenness of slavery. Fowler reports:

Kain't tell you nothin' 'bout 'dem days any more dan dey was Hell—suckin' babies snatch' from dey mudders breas' an' sol' to de specalators. Chillen separated from dey sisters an' brudders, an' never see dem any mo'. Co'se dey cry. You think they not cry when sold off like cattle, goin' inter bondage mo' an' mo', the older dey git? I could tell you 'bout it all day, an' then you kain' even guess 'bout the awfulness of it, belongin' to folks what own you, soul an' body. That can tie you up to a tree, with your face to the tree, an' your arms aroun' it, fastened tight, an' you feet fas'ned too, so you kain't git away, no way, then a long curlin' whip whis'lin aroun' you, cuttin' the blood ever' lick, until folks a mile away hear every lick.[49]

The communal assault inflicted against slaves was incredible, but the violence done to families was exacerbated by the atrocities of physical violence inflicted on individual members of slave communities.

THE GODFORSAKENNESS OF VIOLENCE

The violence inflicted on slaves at the hands of slaveholders and overseers was immense. Howard Thurman explains:

Human slavery has been greatly romanticized by the illusion of distance, the mint julep, the long Southern Twilight, and the lazy sweetness of blooming magnolias. But it must be intimately remembered that slavery was a dirty, sordid, inhuman business.[50]

Physical Violence

While the system of slavery was designed to dehumanize slaves, it appears to have dehumanized many of the slaveholders. Rawick argues that, "American Negro Slavery was a human institution, albeit an exceedingly inhumane one."[51] The inhumane behavior of slaveholders is demonstrated in the cruel physical abuse directed toward slaves. Solomon Caldwell recalls, "Marse Gillam sho was rapid. I saw him whip my mammy till you couldn't put a hand on her shoulder and back widout touching a whelp."[52] Uncle Edd Shirley remembers, "I once saw a light colored gal tied to the rafters of a barn, and her master whipped her until blood ran down her back and made a large pool on the ground."[53]

Susan Dale Sanders adds,

They wo'ked the women and men both in the fields and the children too, and when the ole Master thought they was'n't do'n' 'nuf wo'k, he would take his men and strip off their shirts, and lash them with cow-hide whips until you could see the blood run down them poor niggers backs.[54]

The brutality inherent in slavery was not isolated; severe violent attacks were known throughout slave communities. Wherever slavery existed, violence coexisted. Franklin contends that all slaves were victims of the barbarity of the system. Those who may not have been brutally beaten had to contend with the psychological dynamics in the slaveholder-slave relationship that "stimulated terrorism and brutality because the master felt secure in his position and because he frequently interpreted his role as calling for that type of conduct."[55] One Mrs. Alpheus Lewis "burned her slave girl around the neck with hot tongs." A drunken Kentucky slaveholder dismembered his slave and threw him "piece by piece into the fire." A Mississippi slaveholder beat a slave with more than one thousand lashes because the slave was suspected of theft. Descriptions of runaways used phrases about scars and whipping marks on the body that "suggest a type of brutality that doubtless contributed toward the slave's decision to abscond."[56]

The violence directed toward slaves seemed unreasonable, insane, and demonic. Slaves could find themselves in predicaments impossible to reconcile, leaving them vulnerable to attacks from every side. Sol and Liza Walton report of slaves being whipped until their shirts stuck to their backs and salt water being used to remove the shirts from the skin. For shouting at a white religious meeting, a woman was stripped to her waist and whipped with a bullwhip. Why would slaves face these forms of brutality? According to the Waltons, "Heaps of them was whipped just cause they could be whipped."[57]

Brawley Gilmore relates an event of violence devoid of rationality.

> When I was a boy on de "Gilmore Place," de Ku Klux would come along at night a riding de niggers like they was goats. Yes sir, dey had 'em down on all fours a crawling, and dey would be on dere backs. Dey would carry de niggers to Turk Creek bridge and make dem set up on de bannisters of de bridge; den dey would shoot 'em offen de bannisters into the water. I 'clare dem was de awfulest days I ever is seed. A darky name Sam Scaife drifted a hundred yards in de water down stream. His folks took and got him outen dat bloody water and buried him on de bank of de creek. De Ku Klux would not let dem take him to no graveyard. Fact is, dey would not let many of de niggers take der dead bodies of de folks no whars. Dey just throwed dem in a big hole right dar and pulled some dirt over dem. Fer weeks atter dat, you could not go near dat place, kaise it stink so fer and bad.[58]

When Rebecca Jane Grant was an eight-year-old child, she was once beaten by her mistress because she did not address her mistress's toddler son as "Marse Henry." Grant recalls, "It was a raw cowhide strap 'bout two feet long, and she started to pourin' it on me all de way up stairs . . . she pour it on, and she pour it on."[59]

One woman slaveholder routinely whipped an old female slave. Once the elderly slave went to the slaveholders' greenhouse to work. When the slaveholder determined that her slave had been away too long, she went to the greenhouse to find and discipline the slave. The slaveholder found the elderly slave bending down as if to make a fire. Then she cut her a lick with the cowhide, and lo and behold she was dead. She come running over to our house to get someone to lay her out, and she was crying like she had lost her best friend. Huh, crying because she didn't have nobody to whip no more.[60]

Narratives which recall the cruelties inflicted upon slaves explicitly and implicitly relate a demonic element in the slavocracy. Says Mary Armstrong, "Oh, old Satan in torment couldn't be no meaner than what [William Cleveland] and Old Polly was to they slaves. He'd chain a nigger up to whip 'em and rub salt and pepper on him, like he said, 'to season him up!' "[61]

Harriet Collins explains that the use of salt on the wounds of slaves who had been whipped was "Cose hit hurt lak de bery debbil. Cos hit lef' scars."[62] Anthony Christopher further explains how the injuries sustained from whippings were further aggravated. "I seed dem hold bacon over fire and let de hot grease drop on de bare hide of a nigger what was tie down on de ground and den lash him from de head down to de feet."[63] Easter Jones recalls brutality toward slaves in response to something as insignificant as dropping a dish. "Dey whip you so hard your back bleed, den dey pour salt and water on it. And your shirt stick to your back, so you hadder get somebody to grease it for you kin take it off."[64]

Women faced severe repercussions when they dared to refuse the sexual advances of white men. Minnie Fulkes' mother was beaten because she refused to succumb to an overseer.

Honey, I don't like to talk 'bout dem times, 'cause my mother did suffer misert. You know dar was an' overseer who use to tie mother up in [a] barn with a rope aroun' her arms up over her head, while she stood on a block. Soon as dey got her tied, dis block was moved an' her feet dangled, yo' know couldn't tech de flo! Dis ol' man, now, would start beatin' her nekkid til the blood run down her back to her heels. I took an' seed th' whelps an' scars for my own self wid dese here two eyes (was a whip like dey use to use on horses). It wus a piece of leather 'bout as wide as my han' from little finger to thumb. After dey had beat my mama all dey wanted. . . . Well honey dis man would bathe her in salt and water. Don't you kno' dem places wus a hurtin'.[65]

Pregnant slaves often were shown no kinder treatment than other slaves. The cruelty of overseers and slaveholders found demonic creativity in brutality. "They used to take pregnant women," says Marie E. Harvey, "and dig a hole in the ground and put their stomachs in it and whip them."[66]

Witnesses to the violence inflicted on slaves were inclined to equate the agony of the violence to near-death encounters. Andy Anderson remembers an instance when, after he went to get firewood in a wagon, the wheel hit a stump, the team of animals pulling the wagon jerked, and the wagon's whippletree broke. Anderson's recollection of the following beating and others like it led him to conclude that hell was too good for Master House, the slaveholder.

So he ties me de stake and every half hour for four hours, dey lays ten lashes on my back. For de first couple hours de pain am awful. I's never forgot it. Den I's stood so much pain I not feel so much and when dey takes me loose, I's jus' 'bout half dead. I lays in de bunk two days, gittin' over dat whippin', gittin over it in de body but not de heart.[67]

For an act of violence against her mistress, a mulatto slave named Clory was whipped "until dere wusn't a white spot on her body. Dat wus de worst I ebber see a human bein got such a beatin. . . . I t'ought she wus goin' to die."[68]

Sometimes the physical violence directed toward slaves did result in death.

A woman named Charlotte had real long hair and they cut one side of her hair off and left the other side long. They whipped her one evening for the longest time, and told her to get over the barb wire fence, and she said she couldn't, and he jerked her through by the hair, and she never did come through. She was a corpse in 10 minutes after they jerked her through. I never did know how come her to be beat up like that. But they would beat you for anything.[69]

A San Antonio woman beat her slave until the slave died. "Yessiree, just beat her to death. They say when the woman was beating her, up till the time she died, she just say in a po' moanful voice, 'Oh, pray, Miss Mary.' "[70]

When accounts of violence against slaves do not talk of near-death experiences or actual encounters with death, they often graphically recall the amount of blood spilled by slaveholders and overseers with whips in their hands. Overseers known by Campbell Armstrong would restrain slaves, stretch them on the ground, and whip them.

> If he wouldn't lay down they'd call for help and strap him down and stretch him out. Put one man on one arm and another on the other. They'd pull his clothes down and whip the blood out of him. Them people didn't care what they done since they didn't do right.[71]

Hector Godbold witnessed a slave being struck seventy-five times with a cat-o'-nine-tails. "De blood run down off him just like you see a stream run in dat woods."[72]

William Coleman tells of an occasion when a slave brushed against a mistress while helping her with yard work. While the mistress thought nothing of the light bump against her, the slaveholder took offense and took the slave to a field,

> tied his hands together, throwed the other end of the rope over a limb on a tree and pulled that negro's hands up in the air to where that negro had to stand on his tiptoes, and Maser he took all that negro's clothes off and whipped him with that rawhide whip until that negro was plum bloody all over. Then he left that poor negro tied there all the rest of the day and night.[73]

Psychological Violence

The bloody business of violence against the slaves also ran in another direction. There was a flow of psychological pain that pooled in the lives of slaves. Children were victims of this psychological abuse. They were exposed to the violent beatings of even their own parents. The tragedy witnessed and the helplessness of the moment was a cruel experience slave children had to endure. When Walter Rimm recalls witnessing his father being whipped, he declares, " 'Twarnt nothin' Ise could does 'cept stand dere an' cry."[74] Further, according to Susan Hamilton,

> W'en any slave wus whipped all de other slaves wus made to watch. I see women hung frum de ceilin' of buildin's an' whipped with only supin tied 'round her lower part of de body, until w'en dey wus taken down, dere wusn't breath in de body. I had some terribly bad experiences.[75]

Slaves could find themselves in hopeless predicaments with no way to negotiate their perplexing dilemmas. Marie E. Harvey's mother said

> they had a block to put the colored people and their children on and they would tell them to tell people what they could do when the people asked them. It would just be a lot of lies. And some of them wouldn't do it. One or two of the colored folks they would sell and they would carry the others back. When they got them back they would lock them up and they would have the overseers beat them, and bruise them, and knock them 'round and say "yes, you can't talk, huh? You can't tell people what you can do?" But they got a beating for lying, and they would uh got one if they hadn't lied, most likely.[76]

Another former slave remembers the time her oldest sister accidentally broke a clock. The slaveholder tied a rope around the sister's neck, tied her in the yard, and whipped her for a long time. "There stood mother, there stood father, and there stood all the children and none could come to her rescue."[77]

Some slaves were so psychologically affected that they internalized the brutality of the white slaveholders and mercilessly inflicted pain on other slaves. Jane Johnson recalled, "De overseer was a nigger and de meanest man, white or black, I ever see. Dat nigger would strut 'round wid a leather strip on his shoulder and would whip de others unmerciful."[78]

Violence was confronted from every direction. It was used to manipulate, discipline, and satisfy the perversion of those in control. It was manifested physically and psychologically. All slaves were subject to the physical and psychological violence described here, yet another form of violence was directed specifically at one group of slaves—females. Women and girls knew an expression of Godforsakenness through their victimization by sexual exploitation.

THE GODFORSAKENNESS OF FEMALE SEXUAL EXPLOITATION

All slaves were subject to physical exploitation. A fundamental quality of being a slave is that one has no control over the use of his or her body. However, like contemporary African-American females, female slaves faced an additional dimension of oppression, compared to their male counterparts: sexual exploitation.[79]

Slavery posed a practically insurmountable challenge to the creation and cultivation of relational stability because slave owners dictated the freedom and restrictions imposed on slaves, and male slaves had virtually no authority to defend their wives from physical victimization and sexual exploitation. Slaveholders determined the amount of time spouses could spend together and manipulated the slaves' vulnerabilities for disciplinary purposes. Further, no female slave was safe from the sexual advances of white men. This caused humiliation and dehumanization for both female and male slaves.[80]

The Concubinage of Female Slaves

Female slaves were constantly vulnerable to sexual exploitation, and physical attractiveness was a liability. Richard Macks speaks of "a colored girl, a mulatto of fine stature and good looks" who was taken by a trader to his room "to satisfy his bestial nature." As she resisted, a struggle ensued in which she killed the man. She was consequently charged with murder. Although she was eventually freed, her attack "was the result of being goodlooking, for which many a poor girl in Charles County [Maryland] paid the price."[81]

No female slave family member was safe from the lasciviousness of slaveholders, plantation overseers, and white men in general, and no recourse was available to victims of sexual exploitation. "White males consistently 'broke in' young black girls just arrived into puberty."[82] Slave women were victims of the male lusts of the slaveholding community, and these women would often subsequently bear the wrath of the slaveholders' wives who were scorned by the infidelity of their mates.[83] "I know plenty of slaves (women) who went with the old marster," says one former slave. "They had to do it or get a killing. They couldn't help it."[84] Sexual abuse was extensive and repulsive. In addition to instances similar to those mentioned above, white men would enter slave cabins and rape black women, even in the presence of their husbands.

Sexual exploitation of female slaves was not an uncommon occurrence. Carrie Mason contends, "dat happ'ned a lots in dem days." She goes on to report that white men would instruct their sons to "go down ter dem nigger quarters an' git me mo' slaves."[85] Although some exceptions stand, sexual intercourse between slaveholders and slaves was rarely of mutual consent. The only law slaves knew were the laws of their masters, and since the slaves were considered property, slaveholders imposed themselves on their slaves—they raped them.

In addition to the humiliation of rape, blame was placed on slave women for having been victimized. Zeke Bosman, an overseer, "spoiled a colored girl." Upon the birth of the resultant child, the woman's slaveholder "put her off in a house by herself and wouldn't let her see even her paw and maw."[86]

The manipulation of female slaves was expressed at the will of slaveholders whose domination made avoidance virtually impossible. Mary Reynolds knew a Dr. Kilpatrick who "took a black woman as quick as he did a white and he took any on his place he wanted and he took them often."[87] Despite the alleged Christian convictions of slaveholders, this manipulation and domination continued. Cureton Milling tells of his slaveholder, Levi Bolicks, who would

> take 'vantage of de young gal slaves. "You go yonder and shell corn in de crib," he say to one of them. He's the marster so she have to go. Then he send de others to work some other place, then he go to de crib. He did dis to my very aunt and she had a mulatto boy. . . . Marster was doin' dis devilment all de time and gwine to Presbyterian Church at Salem every Sunday; dat make it look worse to me.[88]

Female Slaves as Breeders

Women were often looked upon as breeders. Sometimes strong men would be "matched" with strong women to increase the likelihood of the conception of healthy, strong slave children. A former slave recalls,

"Whenever a girl had a baby in slavery they never paid no 'tention to it, 'cause they knowed they would have more slaves the more babies they got."[89] A woman who was considered an extraordinary breeder would be advertised as such for sale. Virginia had the distinction of being known to pro-slavery supporters as a "negro raising state," yielding an adequate supply of slaves for itself and thousands for export.[90]

Women forced into sexual surrogacy roles often became pregnant with biracial children called mulattoes. Occasionally these biracial offspring would enjoy a modicum of privilege relative to the children of black parents, but normally they were treated like other slave children. Sometimes they would be sold away to avoid embarrassment to the white slaveholders or their families. Hence it was not uncommon for slaves to admit reluctantly, "My master was my father. . . ."[91] Lucy Galloway's father was the slaveholder of Lucy and her mother. Lucy's mother, Mary, cared for the children of her slaveholder and his wife. The slaveholder's wife was institutionalized because of insanity after giving birth to her fifth child. Subsequently, Mary assumed the sole role of mothering the slaveholder's children as well as her own children. Then the slaveholder sold Mary's husband. Shortly thereafter, Lucy was born. Lucy remembers her mother's explanation of the circumstances around Lucy's conception. "My mother," according to Galloway, "said she couldn't hep herself—dat she wuz jest a slave...."[92]

A male slaveholder would sometimes have two families simultaneously—one with his white wife and the other with his black slave.

> You know when a man would marry, his father would give him a woman for a cook and she would have children right in the house by him, and his wife would have children too. Sometimes the cook's children favored him so much that the wife would be mean to them and make him sell them. If they had nice long hair she would cut it off and wouldn't let them wear it long like the white children.[93]

There were times when slaveholders would forfeit marriage in favor of keeping concubines accessible and available. These concubines were still slaves, and the offspring would likewise be slaves, obtaining their legal status from their mothers rather than their fathers. Speaking of Major Odom, Mrs. Thomas Johns recalls that, "He wuz never married, but he had a nigger woman, Aunt Phullis she was called, that he had some children by. . . . Major Odom treated their children jus' like he treated the other niggers."[94]

Female slaves were unable to escape exploitation from the slave-holding community. They could be repeatedly raped by slaveholders and overseers, tortured for refusing to comply with the sexual demands of their oppressors, and victimized by enraged mistresses who vented their anger and frustration by punishing the exploited slave women.

> Old Marse was de daddy of some mulatto chillun. De 'lations wid de mothers of dese chillun is what give so much grief to Mistress. De neighbors would talk 'bout it and he would sell all dem chillun away from dey mothers to a trader.[95]

Having experienced the brokenness of community through family separations, suffering the violent brutalities inflicted on slaves by slaveholders and overseers, and enduring the victimization of sexual exploitation, African-American slaves encountered the extremities of human suffering. One might suspect that the only sufficient relief for this existential dilemma would be manumission. Yet having lived their entire lives in a racist system intent on humiliation and dehumaniza-tion, how might slaves be equipped to venture into a new system of life without financial resources, adequate education, or capital? While the slaves were set free by the Emancipation Proclamation and the victory of the Union over the Confederate States, what was life to be like for the former slaves? What systems were in place to facilitate their entry into the mainstream of life in the United States during Reconstruction? There were no appropriate provisions made to receive these former slaves into life as free people, so the life that followed enslavement was not as glorious as the former slaves had hoped. Consequently, the forsakenness slaves had known through family separations, violence, and sexual exploitation was extended in a new dimension of anomie in the wake of the dissolution of slavery.

THE GODFORSAKENNESS OF ANOMIE

As southern culture crumbled, the lives of the slaveholding commu-nities were left in disarray, as were the lives of slaves. While clear

demarcations in social customs and practice delimited white southerners' lives from black southerners' lives (whether free or slave), southern
living for whites and blacks was inextricably bound. No significant
changes could occur for slaveholders that would leave slaves unaffected, nor could major adjustments in slave life leave slaveholding
communities untouched. Just as life for former slaveholders would
never be the same, neither would life be unaltered for former slaves.

As long as one was a slave, one understood the nature of society—
norms, expectations, restrictions, and the like. Further, understanding
the rules of society enabled slaves to function, survive, and on rare
occasion thrive. However, after emancipation, social norms were functionally annihilated. Illiterate, poor, and inexperienced in fending for
themselves in an allegedly free society, former slaves were suddenly
no longer enslaved and lived in anomie in the wake of the dissolution
of slavery.

Emancipation: The Answer or a New Question?

Addressing the topic "Twenty-Five Years of Freedmen's Work"
during the fiftieth annual meeting of the American Baptist Home
Mission Society in New York, J. B. Simmons declared: "Slavery was
the cause of the war and emancipation was its cure. . . . The Agony of
the nation's birth-throe is over, and we all rejoice together that five
millions of our African brethren have been born to liberty."[96]

While emancipation changed the status of the African American,
attitudes were not immediately liberated. As much as three decades
after the Emancipation Proclamation, it was observed that "the old
notions and the old animus of the whites concerning the negro were
essentially unchanged."[97] With the war ended, the question arose as to
what the future held. The manumitted slaves were "houseless, penni-
less, without business experience, without capital or credit. . . . The
black man is ground between the upper and nether millstones of
poverty and politics."[98] While many thought freedom was the long-
awaited answer to the problem of slavery, the uncertainties of the future
provided new dimensions of agony.

The Disarray of the Family

Slavery's demise did not automatically make all things good for
former slaves. Their lives had been filled with such havoc that events

subsequent to emancipation reminded them of slavery's cruelty, and many aspects of slavery continued to haunt the former slaves in their newfound lives. Henry Brown tells of a woman whose child was taken from her and sold when the child was eight years old. The slaveholder at the time of the child's birth had a practice of branding the infant slaves when the babies became one year old. After slavery, the woman and her now adult child met and married, unaware of the particularities of their pasts. After a month of marriage, the couple began telling each other of their experiences. "W'en he showed her the bran' she faint' 'cause she then realize' that she had married her son."[99] Other lives were confronted with unimaginable conflict when formerly married couples who had been sold away from each other by slaveholders found each other after manumission. Sylvia Durant says, "dey sold my uncle's wife away en he never didn' see her no more till after freedom came en he done been married again den."[100]

Joanna P. Moore recognized slavery's traumatic effects on family life. Her observation was, "No slave could have a *real* home." While this is an overstatement, inasmuch as her concept of "home" was that of her own privileged upbringing, her point is well taken. Although her work with southern blacks began in 1863, as late as 1913 she confessed, "No pen of mine can picture their desolation. You must imagine."[101] In another place Moore wrote, "Such a mass of suffering, sin and ignorance—surely the world has never before witnessed."[102]

Chaos

The days and years following slavery were chaotic for the newly freed people. One former slave who served with the Union army was robbed after his discharge, losing both his money and his discharge papers. Because he did not know the details of the regiment with which he served, the former slave never secured his pension. Says the veteran, "I would be all right now if I coulda just kept them papers. . . . I sure ought to get something out of it."[103]

At the end of slavery, many manumitted slaves did not know what to do. Where would they go? How would they support themselves and their families? While the former slaves were free to leave the plantations where they had been bound, some stayed. "When the war was over," recalls Virginia Harris, "we stayed right there on the place. We didn't have nowhere to go. We didn't know nothing else but to stay."[104]

Many slaves faced mixed emotions at the conclusion of the Civil War. Great jubilation was known because of the end of chattel slavery. However, incredible angst existed concurrently in the minds and hearts of the former slaves because of the uncertainties that lay ahead. Jerry Howell remembers, "When the war was over and the property all destroyed, and we were told we were free some shouted, some cried and the rest did not know just what to do."[105]

The complex emotions of former slaves concerning the end of slavery was further complicated by a peculiar irony. Union soldiers who had fought the victory that manumitted four million slaves exploited the slaves who were being freed. Annie Coley reports that when Yankee soldiers came and told the slaves of their freedom, the soldiers took two of the four hens that Coley's mother had. They also took Coley's father to the army camp, where he had to clean and cook the hens that had been confiscated.[106]

Life for the former slaves was confusing at every turn. Louis Cain contends that

> this here time after the war between the States had been hell on the poor negro race. . . . If white man don't treat him fair and square the negro cannot say anything, if he does the white people will hang him, so there you are son.[107]

Economic Instability

Economics after slavery afforded minimal opportunity for surviving and virtually no chance for thriving as a former slave. White people suffered economically from the instability of the new way of life, and black people consequently faced an exaggerated instability because of their pragmatic dependence on the economic well-being of the former slaveholding class. Says Lewis Jefferson about life after emancipation, "All de white folks was pore and dey cud not pay de black folks fur work, an' de black folks had no credit an' some uf dem went to stealin' an den de Bull Dozers wud git dem fur dat."[108]

When the slaves were freed, they were told by Yankee soldiers that the government would give them land and a mule or horse with which to farm the land. This gave the slaves hope for a bright future for themselves. This hope, however, soon encountered the stark reality that Elizabeth Finley describes and history verifies, "but we never did git nothing frum dem."[109] Another former slave succinctly expresses the sentiment of many. "White folks will always be hard on niggers and niggers will never have a chance."[110] Eli Coleman believed that when the United States government freed the slaves, part of the slaveholders' properties should have been awarded to the former slaves. Coleman justified this position by arguing that

> everything [the slaveholder] had or owned the slaves made it for him, but we never got anything, just turned us out like a bunch of stray cattle. Had nothing—not even clothes 'cept what we had on our back the day we was freed and our Maser made us stay as we didn't have no other place to go and promised to pay us, but we never did get but very little pay.... Since the negro has been freed it has been hell on the poor old negro. . . . First thing, we was turned loose without anything, no education, not even the way of our people 'cause we had been under the white man rule so long until we had been taken away from our parents.[111]

Andrew Jackson Gill offers a classic expression of the existential dilemma in which many former slaves found themselves following emancipation. While freedom was desired during slavery, sometimes the days of slavery seemed preferable to the difficulties experienced in life as former slaves.

> Sometimes I gits to settin' here a thinkin' back on dem days an' I gits to ponderin', an' I thinks dem slavery days was jes' like human nature. When you has to listen an' work an' do things your missus an' marster say do, you think, "Oh Lord a'mercy, wish I could git off to myself an' do as I please." An' den you is free to go out in de world an' do as you please, you gits to thinkin', "Oh Lord a'mercy, wish I had someone to tell me what to do. I is lost in a fog fer sho'."[112]

Gill has expressed well the condition of manumitted slaves. "I is lost in a fog fer sho'." This "fog" was a sense of confusion, instability, and uncertainty. Former slaves were ill-equipped for the journey ahead and soon to be faced with a racist society that knew slavery was officially ended but was intent on functionally maintaining the status quo. African Americans would still be niggers to the majority of the former slaveholding class. While the black Americans were now sharecropping and working for meager wages, they were still mistreated and abused. They were now free, but they were not free. They were liberated, but they were liberated into an oppressive culture that would continue to hold them in the same disregard as before. God had set them free, but for what? W. E. B. DuBois' poignant inquiry is instructive here:

> Bewildered we are and passion-tossed, mad with the madness of a mobbed and mocked and murdered people; straining at the armposts of Thy throne, we raise our shackled hands and charge Thee, God, by the bones of our stolen fathers, by the tears of our dead mothers, by the very blood of Thy crucified Christ: What meaneth this?[113]

SUMMARY

Christian slaves could reasonably have expected God to manifest Godself in more positive ways in their lives. If God were present, could God not be seen through the stability of strong families? Could God not be believed to deliver from the brutal viciousness of violence? Would not God spare innocent women from the sexual aggression of slaveholders and overseers? Should one not expect freedom to offer more hope than fear, more answers than questions? Christian slaves professed faith in the God of Jesus, but in light of their existential experiences of extreme human suffering, was God present? Had God forsaken these African-American people? DuBois reports that once when Frederick Douglass was a principle speaker at an affair, Sojourner Truth sat in front of the platform and asked a piercing question after Douglass had returned to his seat. "Frederick," called Truth, "is God dead?"[114]

CHAPTER THREE

Godforsakenness in African-American Spirituals

Songs of communities are a vast reservoir of potentiality for theological reflection, discourse, and construction. Songs contain and convey critical theological concepts of various cultures, which is particularly true for the present study. The songs born out of the experiences of antebellum and postbellum African Americans are rich sources of religious questions, convictions, and insight. This is the case of various genres of African-American music, including folk songs, work songs, blues, and spirituals.

While various genres of antebellum and postbellum African-American music offer immense material for analysis, our concern is the theological analysis of spirituals.[1] It must be noted that innumerable spirituals from the antebellum era have been irretrievably lost. The lack of appreciation for this truly American art form contributed to the demise of some. "For more than a century the Negro had been singing his Spirituals before their beauty and significance were in the slightest degree recognized."[2] Agreeing with this sentiment, William Francis Allen, Charles Pickard Ware, and Lucy McKim Garrison commence their commentary on slave songs by observing that "The musical capacity of the negro race has been recognized for so many years that it is hard to explain why no systematic effort has hitherto been made to collect and preserve their melodies."[3]

Thus it is impossible to use the full repertoire of antebellum African-American spirituals. Further, we will not employ a comprehensive collection of the remnant. This study will select representative spirituals that speak to our concerns regarding Godforsakenness and the crucifixion of Jesus. It is significant to note, however, that spirituals addressing these two themes are few in number. The majority of spirituals have themes related to hope, victory, and liberation.

SPIRITUALS AS SOURCES FOR THEOLOGICAL REFLECTION

In the November 8, 1862, edition of *Dwight's Journal of Music* a letter appeared from Lucy McKim, concerning her experience with the music of black slaves. McKim's observations included the following:

> The wild, sad strains tell, as the sufferers themselves never could, of crushed hopes, keen sorrow, and a dull daily misery which covered them as hopelessly as the fog from the riceswamps. On the other hand, the words breathe a trusting faith in rest in the future—in "Canaan's [f]air and happy land," to which their eyes seem constantly turned.[4]

That songs contain significance for the religious concepts and expressions of communities is especially true of communities that embrace Jewish and Christian traditions. Perhaps the classic expression of Jewish and Christian theologies in song is the Book of the Psalms. In both structure and substance, the Psalter stands as a stellar example of a resource for theological insight.[5]

There are two prominent similarities between the psalms of Israel and the spirituals of black Americans. First, both musical forms communicate corporate consciousness. These musical forms do convey individual concerns, but they can in no respect be thought of as individualistic expressions of religious insight. Spirituals, like psalms, are not primarily expressions of personal piety but of communal identity. According to Lawrence W. Levine, the process and structure of spirituals were avenues for individual and communal creativity and expression. Spirituals could be born from slaves observing and sympathizing with the unfortunate circumstances of an individual slave, demonstrating identification and solidarity with the wronged slave. Spirituals referring to the mistreated slave would sometimes be spontaneously created. Additionally, the call and response stylization of spirituals created a dialogue between an individual and the individual's community.[6] Second, both musical forms convey a breadth of human emotion. There is a clear and definite correlation between the emotional intensity found in the words of psalms and spirituals. Just as the Book of Psalms serves as an important source of theology in song, so do spirituals. "While the spirituals reveal the slave's attitude toward his condition in life, they are, like most sacred songs, primarily reflections of his religious concepts."[7] Additionally, African-American spirituals are a significant theological source because of the authenticity of their development from the hearts and souls of African-American people.

The Originality of African-American Spirituals

Slavery took away freedom of movement, relationships, and self-actualization. The one freedom that slaves were able to retain was freedom of thought. While slavery broke the spirits of some, others retained a spiritual and mental tenacity that invoked a buoyancy of heart, regardless of the inhumane system that pervaded every experience of slave life. Music was one avenue expressive of a liberated consciousness amid an oppressed community.

Spirituals convey the sentiments of black slaves. "Songs of sorrow and hope, of agony and joy, of resignation and rebellion, the spirituals were the unique creations of the black slaves."[8] Black spirituals are the unique developments of black people, even though some argue that black spirituals are derivations of white hymns and spirituals. As James Weldon Johnson forcefully argues,

> The statement that the Spirituals are imitations made by the Negro of other music that he heard is an absurdity. What music did American Negroes hear to imitate? They certainly had no opportunity to go to Scotland or Russia or Scandinavia and bring back echoes of songs from those lands. Some of them may have heard a few Scotch songs in this country, but it is inconceivable that this great mass of five or six hundred Negro songs could have sprung from such a source.[9]

That African-American spirituals are a unique art form separate from southern Anglo-American spirituals is firmly established.[10] The complex rhythmic dynamics, call and response style, bodily movement, and repetition are clear indications of the black spirituals' consistency with characteristics of African music.[11] The earliest reference to the distinctive form of African-American spirituals (although the term *spiritual song* was not used for the genre until after the Civil War) is cited in a 1819 complaint of John F. Watson, who describes "a growing evil" of song in public worship "most frequently composed and first sung by the illiterate *blacks* of the society."[12] In an 1899 article in *The Century Magazine*, Marion Alexander Haskell noted:

> Spirituals are the religious songs composed by the negroes themselves, never written or printed, but passing from one generation to another with such additions and variations as circumstances may suggest.[13]

Another indication of the originality of spirituals is their reflection of the historical consciousness and social contexts of slaves.

> The internal and external evidences of slave songs point to conditions under which only negroes lived and died. The exponents of the white-to-Negro song trend were not familiar with the special historical field to which spirituals belong.[14]

The internal evidence is related to the existentialism found in spirituals, the uniqueness of North American slavery as portrayed in the songs, the present world immediacy of spirituals, and the unlikelihood of developing simpler music forms from more complex musical styles. External evidence is related to the development of white choral singing by Virginia Presbyterians in protest to the use of slave songs, the minstrel-like way in which whites sang Negro spirituals, and the condescension with which white singers looked upon the shouting that accompanied Negro spiritual singing.[15]

While some may argue that spirituals are borrowed, it is clear that antebellum African Americans "simply refused to be uncritical recipients of a religion defined and controlled by white intermediaries and interpreters."[16] So while some spirituals may have a relationship to the religious music of white Americans of the slave era, the creation of spirituals remains an authentic form of religious consciousness and expression.

Evidence clearly indicates the originality of African-American spirituals. "The Spirituals are purely and solely the creation of the American Negro; that is, as much so as any music can be the pure and sole creation of any particular group."[17] Not only are black spirituals original products of black people, they also have a particular character.

The General Nature of African-American Spirituals

John Lovell, Jr., advances the idea that the Negro spirituals' generic nature is that of song and folklore. He argues that music has been an integral part of humanity's life, traceable to the most primitive communities.[18] Songs convey something more than individual concepts and concerns. Songs, particularly American black spirituals, possess indications of consciousness that form and inform communities of people. Folklore, like other art forms, is a literary art form that permits communal commentary on the conditions of a particular group of people. Negro spirituals, according to Lovell's research, are a form of folk music that belong to the genre of folklore.

Further, Lovell rightly comments on the holistic character of spirituals. Spirituals bear traditional African traits of attending to life in a universal vis-à-vis a compartmentalized approach. There is no authentic separation in this thought pattern of sacred and secular. Regardless of the presence or absence of conventional religious terminology and phraseology, it is clear that allegedly "secular" songs are saturated with "religious" meaning and "religious" songs are saturated with "secular" meaning.

Every folk song is religious in the sense that it is concerned about the origins, ends, and manifestations of life as experienced by a more or less unified community. Folk songs tend to probe, usually without nailing down definitive answers, the puzzles of life at their roots. The one incontrovertible fact about black spirituals is their African attitude toward religion and music which

> did not splinter into social, political, and philosophical subdivisions. It spoke of the social, the political, and the philosophical with one voice born of the overriding desire to fathom the workings of the universe.[19]

It must be understood that spirituals are more than lyrics and music. A robust appreciation for the impact of spirituals requires witnessing them performed. In addition to the words, rhythms, and harmonies, many spirituals were performed with shouting. Songs were often sung while singers danced in a dramatic "ring shout."

> The shout would start with a leader calling out a verse of a spiritual while the shouters responded by walking around in a circle. When the singers who stood outside the ring took up the chorus, the shout proper would begin with the ring band shuffling rapidly to the beat announced by the hand-clapping and foot-tapping of the chorus of singers who were said then to be "basing" the shouters.[20]

Sterling Stuckey sees an important implication in ring shouts. Ring shouts were no mere theatrical performative addendums to spirituals. According to Stuckey, they have African roots where the circle of the ring has symbolic significance for the community. The ring symbolizes a "circle of culture" that views life as interconnected. This connectedness applies to members of a community as well as to the relationship between present world dwellers and the spirit world. A holism of thought is explicit.[21]

The African impulse toward holism reflected in black music from the antebellum era suggests that religious ideas are discernible from a large collection of songs—spirituals, work songs, blues, and the like. However, since the emphasis of this study is on black spirituals, it is relevant to examine their particular theological quality.[22]

The Theological Legitimacy of African-American Spirituals

Although African-American spirituals do not conform to stylized poetic and musical form and structure, as do the Hebrew psalms, they are no less significant as a source of theology for the people who birthed them than Jewish psalms are for the people who brought them forth.[23] Contrary to some suggestions, the theology of spirituals is not simplistic. It is consistent with the heart of Protestant Christian theology of their era. Olivia and Jack Solomon explain that slave-era spirituals convey

> belief in the omnipotence and omniscience of the one God in tripartite form, in salvation through the crucified Christ, and in

faith-not-works-alone. . . . The spirituals present both a practical and poetic theology.[24]

In his 1894 thesis for Yale School of Divinity, Henry Hugh Proctor offered what is perhaps the first theological analysis of black spirituals by a credentialed African-American theologian.[25] In the thesis, Proctor identifies theological conceptualizations of the doctrine of God, christology, pneumatology, angels, the Christian life, Satan, and eschatology. Proctor's conclusion is that there is a remarkable demonstration of Protestant Christian orthodoxy in the theological concepts of slaves as found in their songs, despite the heretical doctrines to which slaves were exposed.[26]

Proctor identifies another notable quality in the theology of slave spirituals by way of conspicuous absence. For example, nonessential elements concerning christology are nonexistent. Further, even when slaves were exposed to Roman Catholicism, as in Louisiana, they omitted inclinations toward Mariology, despite their Roman Catholic indoctrination. "As far as I can discover by research and experience," says Proctor, "I find no melody of the slave singing divine praises to the Virgin."[27] Proctor concludes that there is observable from the theology of slave spirituals "a tenacious grasp of the fundamental and essential truths of [Protestant] Christianity by these unlettered slaves in the midst of social confusion and moral error. . . ."[28]

Willis J. King recognized the theological significance of spirituals as early as the 1930s.[29] Although several of King's assumptions are faulty, it is significant that he concluded that spirituals were important resources for theology. King argues that the psalms are more "sophisticated" than spirituals because of the psalms' formality of poetry and metrical standards. However, the improvisation, rhythmic intricacies, rich harmonies, and polyphony of spirituals oppose King's argument. Further, the dual usage of phrases and concepts for religious expression and encoded communiques suggests an impressive degree of sophistication in antebellum African-American spirituals. Concerning the dual usage of spirituals, Anne Streaty Wimberly offers a dense explication of how spirituals possess an intricate quality of the use of signs and symbols. Wimberly shows how the "propensity toward signing and symboling in spirituals is especially evidenced in those songs which contain double meanings through secret messages."[30]

King also argues that spirituals have a singular somber background of enslavement and Africanisms had been completely obliterated from the religious conceptualizations of slaves. Clear evidence exists to repudiate King's latter contention, and the statement about the singular background of spirituals relegates slaves' development of spirituals to an exclusively reactionary posture. Doing so ignores the creative circumlocution and imaginative genius in spirituals that demonstrate moments and movements of exceptional independence, in spite of the oppressive conditions of slavery. Using Carl Jung's concept of archetypes, which holds that unconscious material is initially collected as form without content and content evolves through conscious experience, Wimberly explains,

> The symbols which are reflected in the spirituals are at once cultural, ancestral, and universal. They are cultural in the sense that they arose from a specific condition of slavery. They are ancestral in that they were informed by the slaves' African heritage. And, they are universal because they are reflective of the heritage of all men. It may be said that the three kinds of symbols tend to melt imperceptibly into the spontaneous expression of the spiritual.[31]

Despite the problematics of King's analysis in terms of the relative sophistication of spirituals compared to psalms, King rightly acknowledges the religious significance of African-American spirituals, and an adequate appreciation of spirituals requires consideration of their religious content.[32] Further, appreciating spirituals requires attention to their originality as authentic creations of African Americans that contain theological insights from the antebellum era.

The Theological Nature of African-American Spirituals

Levine contends that "The essence of slave religion cannot be fully grasped without understanding [an] Old Testament bias."[33] Songs of New Testament events and personalities are scant. However, according to Howard Thurman, African-American spirituals came forth from the Old and New Testaments, the world of nature, and personal experiences of slaves. Spirituals emerged from slaves' inner lives and the commonality shared with other slaves. The Old and New Testaments, in the imaginative minds of slaves, inspired and illuminated their efforts to discern the mystery of life. Nature provided fertile soil for creative analogy that was concise and simple. The religious experience of slaves was that of consolation and empowerment, solitude and community, sorrow and joy. Spirituals tell of the ultimate realities of slave life from the perspectives of African-American slaves.[34]

In an investigation into the condition of freed people in the Washington, D.C., area in 1862, H. C. Fish of the American Baptist Home Mission Society related a peculiar coexistence of apparently mutually exclusive conditions. On the one hand, he observed, to his surprise, what he defined as "near human beings" who approximate "brutes." This conclusion was reached on his assessment of the former slaves' alleged lack of self-reliance or capacity for self-determination. Further, he inferred that the freed people were devoid of understanding and had no accumulations. On the other hand, Fish argues that "these contrabands are very religious people. They are excitable, impressible, seemingly devout in a very high degree; and there is no doubt, much real piety among them."[35] While one may challenge Fish's qualitative assessment because of his labeling, his impression as to the religious sensitivity and sensibility of the people is obvious from the insights reflected in their spirituals.

Two years after the American Baptist Home Mission Society first sent missionaries to work with southern blacks, the Commission on the Work among the Freed People noted in its 1864 annual report how it found the released people of American oppression: "A people marked in body, mind, and spirit with their long and sorrowful affliction, poor, to absolute destitution, and religiously inclined as only a people divinely prepared are ever found to be."[36]

The idea of manumitted African Americans' divine preparation is not elaborated upon in the report and therefore leaves one uncertain of the commission's intended meaning. It could be an oblique attempt to suggest a providential intent within the experience of slavery. If this is the case, the reference would indicate a Calvinist assumption on the part of the commission's members. Whether the commission's report suggests that something prior to the enslavement of African peoples or the process of enslavement itself had a divine preparatory function is not elucidated. What is indicated here is ambiguous. However, if the commission's observation concerning the religious inclination of African Americans of the era is correct (and the holistic conceptualization discussed above suggests the appropriateness of this conclusion), it is appropriate to move forward with serious examination of the theology born out of the community of African-American slaves and freed people. It is imperative to ascertain something of the theology of slaves through spirituals because spirituals "were created and refined by the slaves themselves as religious and social statements about the context of their lives."[37]

Spirituals reflect slave attitudes toward life, and some argue that spirituals *primarily* reveal reflections on religious concepts. While debates continue as to the primary emphasis on sociology or theology, it is clear that in spirituals one finds the slave seeking redemption by God and communion with God.

> The God of the spirituals was visible in nature, present in the consciousness of man, omnipotent and omnipresent. . . . [God] was no abstraction, but a Being who took an interest in the lowly slave and interceded in his behalf. . . . [God] was the great Comforter.[38]

Nathan Wright, Jr., sees so much theological significance in black spirituals that he makes an audacious projection.

> Indeed, the literature of the spirituals may be said to be—and perhaps in due time will officially or generally be recognized to be—a kind of Third testament, adding a new dimension of hope to the insightful "God encounters" in the present Old and New Testaments.[39]

While Wright's assertion may be ambitious, his underlying assumption as to the significant resource of spirituals for theological investigation is well-founded. Wright identifies theological elements in black spirituals in terms of a channel of contemporary explication of the immanence and transcendence of God, the dynamic liberative activity of God, an anthropological impulse grounded in the *imago Dei*, God's suffering, a christology that embraces the concepts of suffering servant as well as King of Glory, the righteousness and justice of God, and an eschatalogical orientation toward the hope of eternal life in the presence of God, which is radically antithetical to the life of imposed servitude and suffering of slave life.[40]

African-American spirituals articulate theology in relation to the particular social and cultural contexts of African-American people. The black experience "is the story of black life in chains and of what that meant for the souls and bodies of black people," says James H. Cone. "This is the experience that created the spirituals, and it must be recognized if we are to render a valid theological interpretation of these black songs."[41]

African-American spirituals have a rich texture and deep contours that examine all aspects of the human condition—from life, to death, to life after death. Liberation is a prominent theme identified by Cone in the spirituals of slaves. He argues that "divine *liberation* of the oppressed from slavery is the central concept in the black spirituals."[42] Slavery, this argument holds, was irreconcilable and contradictory to the will of God. The Exodus experience; Daniel's deliverance from a lion's den; the rescue of Shadrach, Meshach, and Abednego from a raging furnace; as well as the liberating thrust of Jesus of Nazareth, are reflected in spirituals that testify to the liberation theme of black spirituals. The liberation impulse in antebellum Christian African Americans was so strongly interpreted at times that black abolitionists and revolutionaries interpreted scripture in ways that theologically compelled their opposition to slavery.[43]

> The religious music of the slaves . . . [is] pervaded by a sense of change, transcendence, ultimate justice, and personal worth. The spirituals have been referred to as "sorrow songs," and in some respects they were. . . . But these feelings [of abandonment and trouble] were rarely pervasive or permanent; almost always they were overshadowed by a triumphant note of affirmation.[44]

Further, "For all their inevitable sadness, slave songs were characterized more by a feeling of confidence than of despair."[45]

Appreciating the contextual and universal dimensions of spiritual songs is crucial for appreciating the theology therein.

> The Spiritual is the medium through which the black man made an affirmation of himself as man, and through this medium, he portrayed his existence before God. Although the nature of the language of the Spiritual cannot be separated from the reality in which it participates (slavery), there is a reality   which lies

behind the existence of the language (the historical African consciousness).[46]

Further, spirituals possess images that

transcend the particular time and place of slavery; thus, similar images have occurred throughout the ages in Africa and other areas of the world as persons experienced life and sought meaning. It is this recognition of connection with the history of humankind through the collective unconscious which imbues spirituals with a universal quality.[47]

African-American spirituals offer significant resources for theological analysis from the antebellum African-American Christian tradition. They are rich resources waiting to be probed, analyzed, and understood. Proctor's early treatise on slave songs poignantly articulates the value of mining the theology of spirituals.

Art, heart, and thought are joined in these songs. They are to be admired for their art, loved for their heart, and treasured for their thought. They contain more religious and theological truth than would at first be supposed. Not allowed to formulate his thought in public address, the slave expressed his sentiments in song. These songs were born of necessity; human nature must have an expression. The Negro was ever singing; he sang of his troubles and his hopes, his bondage and his freedom. Mingled with these were echoes of his struggles with sin, his striving after godliness, his fleeing from Satan, his search for God. So that the student, tracing out the intricacies of thought in these songs, in the mind of the slave by no means invalidates the claims of its existence. It is well known that one may speak logically, and yet have no knowledge of logic as a science.[48]

GODFORSAKENNESS IN AFRICAN-AMERICAN SPIRITUALS

While slaves shared common tragedies of their oppression, there was no homogeneous response common to the entire community. Slaves shared the fact that their experience had to be confronted, but they responded to their harsh realities in various ways. According to John E. Taylor,

> Many slaves were dismayed at the situation of their bondage, and confused about their own reactions and possible alternatives, but there was no monolithic "Negro" attiude. There were militant slaves; there were apathetic slaves. Some of them were at times aggressive in their hatred toward the white master, at other times docile.[49]

Further, some slaves rejected Christianity while others were driven to question the justice of God in light of the plight of chattel slavery.

Some slaves responded to their reality with rejection and irreverent parodies of the Christian religion.[50] Other-worldliness was ridiculed:

> I don't want to ride no golden chariot;
> I don't want no golden crown;
> I want to stay down here and be,
> Just as I am without one plea.

Songs of Christian slaves were modified to fit the interpretation of those who had rejected Christianity. "Live humble to the Lord" became to "Live a humbug." "Reign Master Jesus, Reign" was changed to:

> Rain, Mosser, rain hard!
> Rain flour and lard and a big hog head,
> Down in my back yard.

James H. Cone cites Bishop Daniel Payne's account of how difficult it was for some slaves to reconcile divine revelation with human servitude. Slaves would see their slaveholders worshiping, hear the slaveholders professing Christianity, and hear the prayers of slaveholders—while concurrently holding slaves. Slaves recognized the inconsistency of the slaveholders' professions and practices. Cone quotes Bishop Payne:

> A few nights ago . . . a runaway slave came to the house where
> I live for safety and succor. I asked him if he were a Christian;

"No sir," said he, "white men treat us so bad in Mississippi that we can't be Christians."[51]

Some slaves questioned the justice of God. Cone relates Bishop Payne's personal struggles with reconciling the justice of God with the system of slavery. Although Payne was not a slave at the time, it is reasonable to conclude that his questions reflect the insight of others in slave communities.

> I began to question the existence of the Almighty, and to say, if indeed there is a God, does he deal justly? Is he a just God? Is he a holy Being? If so, why does he permit a handful of dying men thus to oppress us? . . . Thus I began to question the Divine government, and to murmur at the administration of his providence. And could I do otherwise . . . ?[52]

All slaves did not unwaveringly subscribe to the Christian notion of an absolutely just and good God. How could they, given their existential realities? The contextual circumstances of antebellum African Americans demanded an authentic articulation of their testimony of God and how God interacted with humanity, especially humanity that had been subjected to inhumane treatment because of slavery.

Life Filled with Trouble

Life for black slaves and freed people was one of intense agony, in spite of the minority report of the goodness of slavery and the slavocracy to which people such as Cora Shepherd testified, "Yessum, I love my white folks!"[53]

Slave life was a life filled with trouble. This trouble came from the disruption of life, which caused uneasiness about one's death. The troublesome nature of life also provoked overwhelming grief manifested in weeping. Beyond the tears, however, the troublesome quality of life in slavery was sometimes so intense and overwhelming that the resultant emotion was one of numbness. Sometimes slaves had cried so long that they had no more tears left to shed.

"I'm in Trouble"

I'm in trouble, Lord, I'm in trouble,
I'm in trouble, Lord, Trouble about my grave.

Sometimes I weep, Sometimes I mourn,
I'm in trouble about my grave;

Sometimes I can't do neither one,
I'm in trouble about my grave.[54]

The troublesome quality of black life in slavery was psychologically disturbing. This does not suggest a condition of neurosis; rather the indication is that one's psychological well-being was continually challenged by constant confrontations with the insanity of slavery. The assaults upon human dignity by the slavocracy were immense and could leave their victims reaching for sane solutions within an insane situation.

"I'm A-Trouble in De Mind"

I am a-trouble in de mind,
O I am a-trouble in de mind;
I ask my Lord what shall I do,
I am a-trouble in de mind.[55]

Both of the above examples clearly indicate the pervasive nature of trouble, which was part of slave life. Further, neither song concludes with a resolution to the dilemmas in which the singers find themselves. It should be noted that while the first selection has no redemptive quality in terms of a resolution to the trouble of life, the second does supply a pointer to Christian slave responses to life's hardships. While trouble is all around and life poses significant challenges to the slave psyche, the singers clearly show a path to a resolution of their problems—asking the Lord what to do.

The Jesus whom the slaves knew was not aloof, impassible, or untouchable. In Christian slave thought, Jesus was the Son of God as well as the crucified, buried, and risen Christ. But Jesus was more. Christian slaves possessed a particular concept of Jesus as a friend, and they understood themselves as enjoying a close and open friendship with Jesus. The friendship was so intimate, slaves even felt comfortable in making demands of their friend Jesus.

> Meet me, Jesus, meet me
> Meet me in de middle of de aiah
>
> So's if my wings should fail me
> Meet me wid another pair.[56]

Since Jesus was a friend of slaves and slaves enjoyed a close relationship with him, there evolved in spirituals a desire to identify with Jesus, who knows trouble and overcomes.

As the following song indicates, trouble was not an occasional disruption of an otherwise placid existence. It was an all-embracing phenomenon, a universal quality of slave life that was inescapable. But perhaps slaves could find temporary respite in Jesus. Further, while community in suffering served as a major sustaining force, slaves might be able to garner sufficient ability to avoid imposing their experiences of trouble onto others, thus becoming a "disturber" to already adequately disturbed members of the slave community.

"All Time Trouble in My Heart"

> Lord, I doan want er be no disturber in my heart,
>   in my heart.
> Lord, I doan want er be no disturber in my heart,
>   in my heart.
> In er my heart,
> In er my heart,
> In er my heart,
> In er my heart,
> Lord, I'm all time in trouble in my heart.
>
> Yes, I want er live lac Jesus in my heart. . . .[57]

Christian slaves looked to Jesus for help in their trouble not out of desperation, but out of faith in Jesus. This faith is not speculation in abstract theological propositions. This faith is grounded in a conviction of Jesus' intimate understanding of slaves because of his immersion in the human condition. Slaves understood Jesus as having known immense suffering, therefore Jesus could appreciate the suffering of slaves in a unique fashion. Jesus' understanding of the agonizing suffering of slaves was thought to be so intimate that he could understand the forsakenness of slaves as no one else could.

"Nobody Knows the Trouble I've Had"

> Nobody knows de trouble I've had,
> Nobody knows but Jesus.
> Nobody knows de trouble I've had,
> Glory hallelu![58]

This song has a peculiar quality. After expressing the conviction that the extent of life's troubles is so extreme that only two can comprehend it—the singer and Jesus—the last phrase is one of praise. Perhaps because someone else is able to identify with the troubles of the singer, the singer is not alone in trouble. Another alternative may be that not only is there someone else who understands the troubles of life, but because that someone is Jesus, there may be a sense of hope for survival and perhaps victory. Whatever the specific implications concerning the identity of the one who experientially appreciates the troubles of slave singers, it is clear that there is particular significance in the identity of the one who understands. That Jesus is the one who knows the troubles of life is of eminent importance.

Another version of this song is found in James Weldon and J. Rosamond Johnson's collection of slave songs. This version agrees that Jesus is the only one who fully appreciates the vexation of life, but there is an important difference: in the second version, there is no expression of praise.

> Nobody knows the trouble I see,
> Nobody knows like Jesus.
> Nobody knows the trouble I see,
> Nobody knows like Jesus.[59]

"Glory Hallelu!" is conspicuously missing from this version. What may be inferred from the absence? Perhaps there is a modicum of comfort in the fact that Jesus does know, as no other can, the trouble of the slave—but there is not yet cause for praise.

Undoubtedly this confidence in Jesus' understanding of the troubles of slave life is related in some way to slaves' understanding of the suffering and death of Jesus. Slaves had an intimate awareness of death.

Death as Integral to Life

Death was not alien to the immediate experience of slaves. Unlike contemporary culture, where people are often to a large degree removed from death, slaves were close to it. Today people die in hospitals and are cleaned and prepared for burial by professionals. Such was not the experience of slaves. They prepared the bodies of deceased loved ones for burial, made the coffins to be used, "kept watch" over the dead in their modest homes, and buried the corpses.[60]

Death was not alien; neither was it shunned. Death was a reality squarely confronted. Sometimes it was reluctantly faced, but at other times it was boldly embraced. Death could be experienced with anticipation, frustration, or relief, but death was directly encountered. For the antebellum African American, there was little fear of death. The black slave spoke of death with familiarity and sometimes fondness.[61]

That slave theology directly considered death's imminence is seen clearly in the song entitled "Shall I Die?"

> Believer, O shall I die?
>   O my army shall I die?
>
> Jesus die, shall I die?
>   Die on the cross, shall I die?
>
> Die, die, die, shall I die?
>   Jesus da coming, shall I die?
>
> Run for to meet him, shall I die?
>   Weep like a weeper, shall I die?
>
> Mourn like a mourner, shall I die?
>   Cry like a crier, shall I die?[62]

It is clear that death is a near reality for the singers of this song. Further, one recognizes the rhetorical nature of the repetition of the question, "Shall I die?" The obvious answer is that death is an inevitable reality of life. Just as Jesus died, the slaves would die. Further, the reality of death is indicated in that members of the community knew what it was to weep and mourn the death of others. Therefore, at the death of the singer of this song, weepers and mourners would know to respond, as they had responded to death before. Additionally, Allen, Ware, and Garrison note that occasionally the lead singer of this song would repeat the words, "Die, die, die" mournfully.[63] It is clear that death was a well-known companion to slaves.

Since death was such an intimate acquaintance, slaves would indicate the manner in which they wished to die. Death was certain, and Christian slaves could encourage one another to die with dignity. This meant to die as Jesus died. This is seen in the song "Lord, Remember Me," where one verse says:

> If you want to die like Jesus died
>   Lay in de grave,
> You would fold your arms and close your eyes
>   And die wid a free good will.[64]

Death was not an enemy from which one attempted to flee; it was a reality firmly established in the context of human existence. Therefore one could demonstrate character similar to that of Jesus by the way in which one walked through the experience of death.

The harshness of trouble and death can sometimes be seen tempered by the slaves' intimacy with Jesus. However, some spirituals seem without this residue of confidence in the salvaging of life's hardships.

The Hopelessness of Life

Certain spirituals hold obvious signs of resignation to the hopelessness of life. Sometimes this seemingly hopeless existence moves from the bleakness of the singers' lives to the bleakness of the death encountered by Jesus. Life will bring bleakness, and one can be challenged to anticipate how the bleakness will be met.

"What Yo' Gwine to Do When Yo' Lamp Burn Down?"

O, po' sinner, O, now is yo' time
O, po' sinner, O, what yo' gwine to do
 when yo' lamp burn down?

Find' de Eas' fin' de Wes',
What yo' gwine to do when yo' lamp burn down?
Fire gwine to burn down de wilderness,
What yo' gwine to do when yo' lamp burn down?

Head got wet wid de midnight dew . . .
Mornin' star was a witness to . . .

Dey whipp'd Him up an dey whipp'd Him down . . .
Dey whipp'd dat man all ovah town . . .
Dey nailed His han' an dey nail'd His feet . . .
De hammer was heard on Jerusalem street. . . .[65]

It is clear in this song how pervasive is the feeling of bleakness. There is no ray of hope concerning a redemptive resolution to one's lamp burning down. An honest exegesis of the text suggests that the certainty of slaves' lamps burning down (and subsequently burning out) is related to the extinguishing of the lamp of Jesus in his crucifixion.

The song "Cry Holy" is another clear example of the despair in which slaves sometimes lived. Until the very last verse there is little, if any, suggestion of hope.

Cry holy, holy!
 Look at de people dat is born of God.
And I run down de valley, and I run down to pray,
 Says, look at de people dat is born of God.

When I get dar, Cappen Satan was dar . . .
Says young man, young man, dere's no use to pray . . .
For Jesus is dead and God gone away . . .
And I made him out a liar and I went my way . . .

O, Mary was a woman, and [s]he had a one Son . . .
And de Jews and de Romans had him hung . . .

And I tell you, sinner, you had better had pray . . .
For hell is a dark and dismal place . . .
And I tell you, sinner, and I wouldn't go dar! . . . [66]

Here is insight as to God's absence in relation to Jesus' death, at least from the testimony of "Cappen Satan," who set out to discourage the suffering slave from praying. However, the slave proves the false-hood of Satan's deceptive ploy and proceeds to seek God amid the slave's struggles. Even so, there is the observation that Jesus' fate was real, with the responsibility for the crucifixion being attributed to both the Jews and Romans. Finally, the ray of hope present here is an admonition to the sinner to avoid the dark and dismal place of hell, which the saved slave contends should be avoided at all cost.

Related to the sense of hopelessness is a longing for relief that would not come.

"De Blin' Man Stood on de Road an' Cried"

O, de blin' man stood on de road an' cried
O, de blin' man stood on de road an' cried
Cryin' O, my Lord, save-a me
De blin' man stood on de road an cried.

Cryin' dat he might receib his sight . . .[67]

Thurman explains the slaves' treatment of the biblical story refer-enced here, in which Jesus heals a blind man. In the biblical story, the blind man longs to see. As he calls to Jesus, his prayer is answered and he receives his sight. Thurman tells how the slaves "identified them-selves completely with the blind man at every point but the most crucial one. In the song the blind man does not receive his sight."[68] It is clear why the slaves would sing the song this way. Just as they had not received freedom, the man in their song had not received sight. There is no evidence to indicate a revision of the song following emancipa-tion.

The sense of hopelessness demonstrated in these spirituals invites a question as to the possibility of hope in fellowship with other slaves. While one may assume that fellowship offered constant hopeful companionship, certain spirituals indicate the opposite. Sometimes the sense of aloneness and abandonment was intense, regardless of who shared the agony of slavery.

The Abandonment of Slave Life

In contrast to the myth that slaves were constantly happy, dancing, and singing is the lucid evidence that slaves knew well the piercing reality of abandonment. One is made acutely aware, by spirituals that speak of the ordeal, of the torment of losing family members.

"Dis Ole World Is Er Mean World"

Dis ole world is er mean world to try to live in,
To try ter stay in until you die.
Without er mother
Without er father
Without er sister, Lord,
Ain't got no brother.

You got ter cry sometime . . .
You got ter pray so hard . . .
You got ter mourn so hard. . . .[69]

While the above song is an example of how slaves could be stripped of every familial relationship, more prominent is the theme of pain from the separation from one's mother. The fracture of the maternal bond appears in a significant way in spirituals. Whether the loss of the relationship between mother and child was through the selling of slaves or the invasion of death into the family circle, the pain of this loss is acute.

"All the Friend I Had Dead en Gone"

All the friend I had,
All the friend I had,

> All the friend I had,
> Dead en gone.
>
> Weepin Mary, weep no longer,
> All the friend I had,
> Dead en gone.
>
> My poor mother died er shoutin,
> All the friend I had,
> Dead en gone.
>
> Gone to the grave yard
> Gone to the grave yard
> All the friend I had,
> Dead en gone.[70]

There is a strange mixture of emotions in this song. On the one hand, there is personal grief that the singer's only earthly friend is "dead en gone." On the other hand, the fact that the mother died a victorious death, as indicated by the instruction not to weep and the recollection of the mother's shouting in her dying, offers a note of consolation. Even so, the singer's only friend on earth is gone.

Perhaps the most recognizable spiritual that attends to the abandonment of slave life is the song "Sometimes I Feel Like a Motherless Chile," which takes up the experience of losing one's maternal bond and applies it to the general experience of life.

> Sometimes I feel like a motherless chile,
> Sometimes I feel like a motherless chile,
> Sometimes I feel like a motherless chile,
> Far, far away from home,
> A long, long ways from home.
>
> Sometimes I feel like I'm almost gone . . .
> Then I get down on my knees an' pray
> Get down on my knees an' pray.[71]

According to Christa K. Dixon, the phrase "I feel like a motherless chile," replaced the African idiom "my father is dead" as the identity of slaves evolved from an African orientation toward a more American consciousness. "My father is dead" was an expression born of African patriarchal society, where the father provided the necessities of life. Thus the saying indicates an existential crisis of living without the person who provided the necessary support for sustaining life. Further, one's father needed not be physically dead for the phrase to have had currency. With the forced termination of paternal relationships among slave families through the slave trade, mothers became the dominant source of provision and security, and motherhood evolved as the dominant symbol for security and survival. The expression "I feel like a *mother*less chile" indicates the extremities of desperation. The second stanza indicates that "the separation and homesickness have become virtually unbearable." The final expression of praying restores the awareness of being a "chile of God."[72]

> In a few sparse lines the spiritual sketches such a vivid picture of a despairing, homesick person that it invites anyone in similar circumstances to identify with it, and to express his or her longings and sorrow through this deeply moving song.[73]

The depth of sorrow encountered by the singers of this spiritual is further intensified by an inclusion found in this song by Marion Alexander Haskell. Haskell's rendition includes a third verse that communicates the depth of pain in slave life with perspicuity: "Sometimes I wish dat I nebbah been bawned. . . ."[74]

Suffering Tempered by Hope

Thurman argues that two profound theological insights are found in the slave spirituals: life is its own restraint, and life's contradictions are not ultimate. He sees in the theology of spirituals an awareness that the economy of life demands that one reaps that which one sows, yet the enslaved were not culpable for their enslavement. This reciprocity of created order is unavoidable. For the enslaved, the ruin of the South after the Civil War was a vindication of the victimization to which they had been subjected. Further, if life's contradictions were ultimate, then life would be fixed in fatalistic, agonizing inevitables. But life's contradictions are not ultimate in this theology. Life is open to an always emerging edge that gives humanity hope for the future.[75] "There is

desolation, fear, loneliness, but hope, at once desperate and profound!"[76]

> In attempting to make sense out of their individual lives, the
> slaves . . . found meaning in their religion. The meaning was not
> so much an answer to the problem of suffering as the acceptance
> of the sorrow and the joy inherent in the human condition and an
> affirmation that life in itself was valuable.[77]

This blend of sorrow and joy is present in "Lis'en to de Lam's."

> Lis'en to de lam's, all a cry-in . . .
> I wan'ta go to heaben when I die.
>
> Come on sister wid yo' ups an' downs . . .
> De angel's waitin' for to give you a crown . . .
>
> Come on mourner an' a don't be shame . . .
> Angel's waitin' for to write-a yo' name.[78]

Here one sees a hope in heaven that survives the onslaught of
slavery's actualities. There is the longing for heaven upon the inevita-
bility of death. There is the invitation to the sister who encounters the
vicissitudes of life, encouraged by the certainty of a reward for a
faithful journey. The ordinary causes for shame in this world are
dissipated when compared to the place of honor afforded by the angel's
waiting to write one's name.

There is a similar admixture of suffering and hope in "My Father,
How Long?" As the question of endurance is placed, the answer comes
in the assurance that liberty is the goal for which to strive.

> My father, how long,
> My father, how long,
> My father, how long,
> Poor sinner suffer here.
>
> And it won't be long . . .
> Poor sinner suffer here.

We'll soon be free . . .
De Lord will call us home.

We'll walk de golden streets . . .
Of de New Jerusalem.

My brudders do sing . . .
De praises of de Lord.

We'll fight for liberty . . .
When de Lord will call us home.[79]

A confident hope is portrayed in this spiritual, in spite of the excessive suffering of life. The problem of bondage will be eliminated by the liberty that lies beyond the grave. Slavery could bind the body but not the spirit of antebellum African-American Christians.

Life is interpreted in different ways in spirituals. Sometimes it is lonely and discouraging, sometimes evil, frustrating, and despairing, sometimes a pilgrimage toward God with death as an integral aspect of the journey of life. However, Thurman's assessment of the significance of spirituals is:

They express the profound conviction that God was not done with them, that God was not done with life. The consciousness that God had not exhausted His resources or better still that the vicissitudes of life could not exhaust God's resources, did not ever leave them. This is the secret of their ascendancy over circumstances, and the basis of their awareness of the presence of a God who was personal, intimate and active was the central fact of life and around it all the details of life and destiny were integrated.[80]

W. E. B. DuBois offers an important conclusion concerning the overarching quality of spirituals.

Through all the sorrow of the Sorrow Songs there breathes a hope—a faith in the ultimate justice of things. The minor cadences of despair change often to triumph and calm confidence. Sometimes it is faith in life, sometimes a faith in death, sometimes assurance of boundless justice in some fair world beyond. But whichever it is, the meaning is always clear: that sometime, somewhere, men will judge men by their souls and not by their skins.[81]

THE CRUCIFIXION OF JESUS IN AFRICAN-AMERICAN SPIRITUALS

Sterling Brown contends that "the best expression of the deepest thoughts and yearnings" of the slaves is found in the spirituals.[82] John W. Work is of similar opinion, especially in spirituals concerning the crucifixion. "In my opinion these black singers reached the pinnacle of noble expressiveness and dramatic description in the tragic, beautiful, poignant portrayal of the crucifixion."[83] If this is true, then the spirituals can inform one's understanding of the response of many Christian slaves to their experiences of forsakenness.

Identification with the Crucifixion

The spirituals that speak of the crucifixion show the clearest relationship between the slaves' forsakenness and that of Jesus while on the cross. This may be because of the accessibility of Jesus to the minds and hearts of slaves. Slaves were confident that Jesus understood them because he knew misery, anguish, and violent death in his own life. Slaves identified with Jesus because, in their perception, he identified with slaves in a particular way. Slaves could resonate with the agony of Jesus and demonstrated their comprehension of the crucifixion in song.

"Crucifixion"

> Dey crucified my Lord,
>   An' He never said a mumbalin' word.
> Dey crucified my Lord,
>   An' He never said a mumbalin' word.
> Not a word—not a word—not a word.
>
> Dey nailed him to a tree . . .
> Dey pierced him in de side . . .

De blood came twinklin' down . . .
He bow'd his head an' died. . . .[84]

Lovell supplies a verse at the beginning of this spiritual that says,
"Oh, dey whupped him up de hill. . . ."[85] One notices the vicious quality
of the song, with which slaves undoubtedly identified by personal
experience or observation. It is apparent that the slaves keenly understood the cruelty, horror, and tragedy of the cross of Jesus Christ, as is
seen in the song "Hammering."

They crucified my Lord . . .
They nailed him to the tree . . .
You hear the hammers ring . . .
The blood came trickling down . . .
Those cruel people! Hammering![86]

The constancy of the slaves' identification with the crucifixion is
seen in the spiritual "Calvary." The crucifixion of Jesus was not
something that had passing significance for slaves. It touched the
pathos of slave thought.

Ev'ry time I think about Jesus . . .
Sho'ly He died on Calvary.

Make me trouble thinkin' 'bout dyin . . .
Sho'ly He died on Calvary.[87]

The immediacy of their sympathy with the passion of Jesus caused
a physical reaction, as seen in "Were You There?"

Throughout two thousand years God's love has been crucified,
hanged, murdered, quenched, suffocated, gassed, bombed millions of times over, in everybody's lifetime, and *nobody* can deny
having been there.[88]

"Were You There?"

Were you there when they crucified my Lord?
Oh! Sometimes it causes me to tremble, tremble,
    tremble.

> Were you there when they crucified my Lord?
> Were you there when they nailed Him to the tree? . . .
> Were you there when they pierced Him in the side?...
> Were you there when the sun refused to shine? . . .
> Were you there when they laid Him in the tomb?...[89]

Attention to the Agony of the Crucifixion

While most churches to which slaves had been exposed displayed empty crosses, slave spirituals give significant attention to the torment of the cross. This spiritual enumerates the agonizing torture to which Jesus was subjected. The repeated inquiry, "Were you there?" forces each person to acknowledge his or her participation in the sin that caused Jesus to die.

> The lyrics of this powerful spiritual, which makes us both wince in shame and rise to our responsibility, seem to belong to a repertoire of succinct formulations into which the Gospel accounts of Jesus' passion have been crystallized by the empathetic faith of many believers. The verses are so compact and polished in their formulation of the highlights of this deeply moving story that they could easily be "learned by the heart" and "kept by the mind" and thus reappear whenever somebody intoned a song on the crucifixion or resurrection having roughly the same rhythmic pattern.[90]

In the song "Were You There?," there is emphasis on the words *you* and *my*. The inquiry has to do with what one was doing if one was present at the crucifixion of "my Lord." Certainly, one would not only watch. The unspeakable, unthinkable, unbelievable neglect "causes me to tremble." According to Lovell's analysis:

> The setting, the phrasing, the powerful momentum of this poem surely make it one of the great poems of all time. Every great wrong, it says, is committed under the eyes of frightened or uncaring people. For the wrongs of humankind, the finger points to us all. We are all guilty. We are guilty not so much because of

what we do, as what we allow to happen. And without a doubt, the slave singer was including slavery of human flesh in the bill of indictment.[91]

Lovell's conclusion is reinforced by his inclusion of verses that confess, "I uz dere win dey nailed 'im to der cross. . . ."[92]

It is important to note the manner in which many of these spirituals about the crucifixion end. They normally end with Jesus dying, dead, or buried. There are selections that focus on the crucifixion and end in the resurrection, but they are rare. This does not suggest that the slaves were resigned to accept their lives in slavery without protest. Instead the songs indicate the intimacy and intensity with which the slaves related to the agony of the crucified Jesus.

For the slave, freedom was not on the horizon; there stretched ahead the long road down which there marched in interminable lines only the rows of cotton, the sizzling heat, the riding overseer with his rawhide whip, the auction block where families were torn asunder, the barking of the bloodhounds—all this, but not freedom.[93]

Antebellum African Americans encountered extremities of human suffering. They communicated a sense of identity with the suffering of Jesus through their spirituals. The spirituals examined thus far not only speak to the general concept of the suffering and crucifixion of Jesus, they hold important implications for understanding Godforsakenness in antebellum African-American theology.

THEOLOGICAL IMPLICATIONS CONCERNING GODFORSAKENNESS

Christian slaves lived closely to God, and from the testimony of a former slave, "God lived close to them, too. Some of them old slaves composed the songs we sing now."[94] The sense of God's living closely to slaves is an important theological conclusion for a study of Godforsakenness in slave thought. Further, its implications are critical for any conclusion as to the theological conceptualization of God's absence or presence in the midst of abject human suffering.

Theological Holism

Thurman sees what he identifies as "the gothic principle of human life" in spirituals.

> It is the recognition of a two dimensional character of reality: the giant gothic cathedral, its pillars grounded firmly in the earth and its awe-inspiring vault reaching toward the heavens. Here is the time-bound and timeless; the finite and the infinite; the particular and the universal.[95]

Despite claims that African belief systems were primitive and unenlightened, these systems show depth and insight often previously ignored. Further, African slaves and their descendants were not completely divested of their African religious influences.

> The traditional religions of Africa have a single overarching characteristic that survived in an attenuated form for generations—a powerful belief that the individual and the community were continuously involved with the spirit world in the practical affairs of daily life.[96]

Religious conceptualizations of black slaves were significantly influenced by West African religious convictions. Among the theological insights of West Africa was the concept of God as essentially spirit with transcendent power and immanent presence. God's presence is constant among humanity, and God is involved with the affairs of God's creation. God is also considered omnipotent, thereby allowing humanity the possibility of achievements. Further, God is compassionate toward the victims of the world.[97]

The Africanisms in slave thought facilitated slaves' ability to relate to classical Christian theology's trinitarian concept of the doctrine of God. West Africans understood the gods to "interpenetrate each other and appear to lack fully discrete identities."[98] West African people of Yoruba had a god called *Elegba* or *Legba*, an important deity who brought divinity to earth, intervening in people's lives and serving as a messenger of the gods. He was similar to Hermes in Greek thought.[99] Legba and the Holy Spirit became similar in concept, because both maintained a link between humanity and the other world. Thus, without contradiction, slaves conceptualized the interrelatedness of Father (or Parent), Son (or Savior), and Holy Spirit (Legba), and some elements of the devil.[100]

The West African concept of the interrelatedness of divinity that influenced antebellum African-American theology is similar to the trinitarian theology of Jürgen Moltmann. In *The Trinity and the Kingdom*, Moltmann articulates a social doctrine of the trinity in which God is a community of Father, Son, and Spirit. The unity of this divine community is found in its constitution of mutual indwelling and reciprocal interpenetration. Moltmann structures this concept in terms of community and relationship versus separation and isolation. He argues the necessity of the social construct to avoid the otherwise inescapable heresies of Arianism (subordinationism) and Sabellianism (modalism). In this framework, the immanent and economic trinity merge into one another to form community. The divine nature of the trinity is that each trinitarian person exists in relation to one another. The unity exists in the circulation of divine life that they fulfill in relation with one another. This is not *filioque* (the Spirit proceeding from the Son), or hypostasis (three persons with homogeneous modes), but perichoresis (at-oneness in relationship), in which the triune God experiences Godself.[101]

The West African concept of the interrelatedness of God went beyond systematic theological conceptualizations of trinity. There was a logical conceptualization of the simultaneous existence of good and evil, the other world and this world.[102] In terms of suffering, it would be reasonable to conclude that slaves could interpret the absence and presence of God simultaneously.

The Presence and Absence of God

Antebellum African Americans experienced Godforsakenness. The existential reality of Godforsakenness is incontrovertible. There were times when it appears that they could not find God in the midst of their suffering and pain. Elizabeth A. Johnson forcefully makes this point from a feminist theological perspective.

> Holy Wisdom does not abhor the reality of women but identifies with the pain and violence that women experience on the cross,

of whatever sort. So we may ask again Elie Wiesel's terrifying question ["Where is God?"]. When a woman is raped and murdered, what does the Shekinah say? She says, my body is heavy with violation. Through the long night when the Bethlehem concubine is gang-raped and tortured, where is God? She is there, being abused and defiled. There too being burned to death by the Inquisition. There too being tortured by the male enforcers of unjust rule. Along with all abused women these women are *imago dei*, *imago Christi*, daughters of Wisdom. Sophia-God enters into the pain of women whose humanity is profaned and keeps vigil with the godforsaken for whom there is no rescue. In turn, their devastation points to the depths of the suffering of God. There is no solution here, no attempt at theoretical reconciliation of atrocity with divine will. Only a terrible sense of the mystery of evil and the absence of God, which nevertheless may betray divine presence, desecrated.[103]

There was, however, another reality that existed concurrently: God was present. With this realization, slaves transcended their circumstances, as seen in the glimpses of hope throughout the majority of spirituals. Antebellum African Americans and their postbellum counterparts sensed that God was present with them even while they were living in the whirling vortex of Godforsakenness.

Eberhard Jüngel offers a contemporary articulation of the absence and presence of God that corresponds to the antebellum African-American concept. Jüngel argues that one needs to learn how to conceptualize God's omnipotence as the withdrawal of God's omnipresence. Correspondingly, one also needs to think of God's omnipresence in terms of God's withdrawal of God's omnipotence. This is the systematic goal of *God as the Mystery of the World*.[104] He argues that one's withdrawn state is essential to one's person. This is especially true with God. While absolute presence is obliterated by one absence, God's presence is exclusively known simultaneously with God's absence. Consequently, revelation is essential for God to be known. Since God's essence is explicitly known through revelation, revelation is integrally related to the connection between presence and absence. For Jüngel, either God must be declared dead, or our thinking of God demands renewal.

Jüngel frames the issue of the question, "Where is God?" cogently. He contends that either the question results negatively in the notion of God's nonbeing, which effectively ends all talk about God, or the question has a positive response that becomes a hermeneutically fundamental question.[105]

Following the thought of Dietrich Bonhoeffer in *Letters and Papers from Prison*, Jüngel agrees with the idea that God allowed Godself to be "pushed out of the world," yet "bears the world on the cross as the world which will not bear him. . . ." The resultant conclusion is that God "explodes the alternative of presence and absence." What this means is that presence and absence are not diametrically opposed. They are taken up into the person of God as being "present as the one who is absent in the world. . . ." Bonhoeffer and Jüngel see the significance of this concept in terms of soteriology as it is related to the cross event.[106]

That the person of God absorbs the idea of presence as absence is analogous to the quality of "removedness" that belongs to the human experience. Wolfhart Pannenberg agrees with this concept and elucidates the idea by referring to concepts of presence, concealment, and personal being. Integral to the personhood of humans is the fact that humans are not totally existent for other humans. The freedom within the personhood of humans means that they can conceal part of their being. They are also free to disclose themselves.[107] Hence the freedom of God permits God to reveal and conceal Godself. If God could not be concealed, God would not be free. If God were not free, God would not be God.

Further, the theology of antebellum African Americans has implications for the question of whether God suffered with Jesus and consequently whether God suffers with God's creatures who endure the inhumanity of humanity. Three essential elements present in this theological construction are: 1) God is both transcendent and immanent; 2) God is present in the midst of the existential experience of absence encountered by suffering humanity; and 3) there is no evidence that antebellum African Americans made an ontological distinction between God as Father and Jesus Christ as God's beloved Son. This theological conception includes the implication that as Jesus suffered in his death and as humans go through the extremities of human suffering, God suffers with God's creation. In contemporary theology, the concept of Godforsakenness is generally represented by three models: 1) Jesus was not forsaken, and God did not suffer;[108] 2) Jesus was forsaken, but God did not suffer;[109] and 3) Jesus was forsaken, and God did suffer.[110] Antebellum African-American theology agrees with the third model.

CHAPTER FOUR

The Godforsakenness of Jesus in Mark's Gospel

In the narrative of the death of Jesus in the Gospel of Mark, Jesus is reported to have uttered only one phrase from the time he gave Pilate a short answer to the question of his identity as King of the Jews (15:2) through his death on the cross. This peculiar silence sharply contrasts with the otherwise substantial speech of Jesus. Further, the nature of Jesus' sudden burst seems inconsistent with the previous indications of the unique and intimate communion he enjoyed with God (e.g., 1:1, 11). When Jesus' awkward silence is interrupted, it is shattered by the piercing cry *"Eloi, Eloi, lama sabachthani?,"* interpreted as "My God, my God, why hast thou forsaken me?" (15:34).

Jesus' cry of dereliction demands theological reflection. However, attempting to discern the meaning of this cry by considering it apart from the rest of Mark's passion-resurrection narrative and the even broader context of the whole gospel narrative seems problematic. Comprehending a portion of a story within its context without imposing one's preconceptions is a challenging task. Attempting to understand an utterance removed from its narrative context leaves one exceptionally vulnerable to the imposing of one's own preconceived notions. Events, characters, comments, and other elements of a narrative are best understood within the context of the narrative in which they are found. Therefore we will proceed with a narrative interpretation of Jesus' cry of dereliction in relationship to the larger Markan narrative, giving appropriate consideration to the theological framework concerning Godforsakenness in antebellum African-American theology.

Approaching a text with the right question is crucial to biblical interpretation. Many readers come to biblical texts asking, "What happened?" This is the wrong question. The right question to ask about the Gospel of Mark, according to R. Alan Culpepper, is radically different: "What did the death and resurrection of Jesus mean to Mark?" Culpepper goes on to contend that as one listens to the text and allows the Gospel of Mark to interpret itself, one will recognize "that the shadow of the cross falls across the entire Gospel so that every pericope points ahead to the cross and must be understood in its light."[1]

While the larger question concerning the meaning of the death and resurrection of Jesus is not the explicit concern of this study, the related concept of the presence or absence of God is apropos. Since the "shadow of the cross" is related to the entire gospel and the question of God's presence is integral to the experience of the cross, the question of God's presence is related to the entire Markan narrative. Therefore the relationship between Jesus and his followers can be seen as a paradigm for interpreting the relationship between God and Jesus.

THE FOLLOWERS OF JESUS: A PARADIGM OF THE PRESENCE AND ABSENCE OF GOD

Attending to the narrative roles of characters in a story is a profitable approach to studying Mark. While various characters could be studied, the followers of Jesus serve as a paradigm for God's presence and absence to Jesus within the narrative. Robert C. Tannehill explains that the disciples appear early in Mark as close companions of Jesus who play a continuing role throughout the Markan account. That the disciples are so prominent in the story invites attention to their role in the story, as it involves their relationship to Jesus. Tannehill observes that Mark introduces the disciples as responding positively to Jesus. This presentation, in effect, "hooks" the reader by inviting him or her to identify with the loyal disciples. However, after Mark draws the reader into the story by identification with the faithful disciples, he begins to present the disciples in conflict with Jesus, which reveals the disciples' inadequacies. Finally, the disciples are portrayed as "disastrous failures." The purpose of this is "to awaken his readers to their failures as disciples and call them to repentance."[2]

Tannehill's proposal of this reading of the disciples is constructive and differs from other interpretations in two ways. Some views argue that the disciples' struggles stem from the fact that the crucifixion and resurrection have not yet occurred in the story. The disciples do not have the advantage of the readers of the text, who live in the light of the resurrection. The resurrection, the argument goes, solves the dilemma of discipleship for those who read the text. However, Tannehill contends that the passion of Jesus does not resolve the disciples' dilemma. Instead, the passion intensifies the dilemma because it calls on the disciples to take up the cross (8:34) and become slaves to all (10:44). Tannehill's proposal is distinctive because he does not see the disciples in a negative light. Those who perceive the disciples negatively sometimes claim they represent a particular element within the church. Tannehill notes that Mark often presents the disciples positively (e.g., 1:16-20; 3:13-19; 6:7-13).[3]

Tannehill's primary focus is on the twelve disciples of Jesus, but other followers of Jesus in the narrative are also disciples. That the male followers of Jesus are directly identified as disciples in no way elevates them above the status of the females who follow him. As the story clearly reveals, one's title does not make one a disciple. On the contrary, one's demonstration of loyalty through actions in relationship to Jesus is the criterion for discipleship.

Presence Prior to the Passion-Resurrection Narrative

Mark presents both favorable and unfavorable characterizations of the twelve disciples of Jesus. Loyalty, misperceptions, resistance, and fear are all part of the character of the disciples in Mark's gospel.[4] Early in the gospel, the disciples display impressive degrees of loyalty. When Mark recalls Jesus' first invitation to men to follow him (1:16-20), they respond affirmatively and immediately. This is significant because the two sets of brothers introduced—Peter and Andrew, James and John— are engaged in their vocation of fishing. That these four men immediately accept Jesus' invitation to leave their current vocation and accept the life of discipleship is commendable. It indicates an intimacy of relationship between leader and followers that is indicative of their presence to him.

A sense of the presence of the disciples to Jesus is also apparent when he calls those whom he desires and appoints twelve men to "be with him, and to be sent out to preach . . . " (3:13-19). Jesus calls, and the men respond. The relationship is not exclusively grounded in working for Jesus; crucial to the relationship between Jesus and his twelve appointees is that they might "be with him."

A third example of the presence of the disciples to Jesus is found in 6:7-13, when Jesus calls his twelve followers, sends them out in pairs, and gives them authority over unclean spirits. That Jesus calls the twelve and sends the twelve is important, but of equal significance is the fact that the authority of Jesus goes out with those who go forth in his name. That the authority of Jesus accompanies the disciples is yet another indication of presence between Jesus and his disciples.

Absence Prior to the Passion-Resurrection Narrative

In spite of the above examples of closeness between Jesus and his disciples, some scholars view the disciples with consternation. Theodore J. Weeden, Sr., interprets Mark as offering a severe critique of the disciples. Because of great dissonance between the christological concept of Jesus and his disciples, the argument follows, Mark portrays the disciples with negativity. Says Weeden:

> I conclude that Mark is assiduously involved in a vendetta against the disciples. He is intent on totally discrediting them. He paints them as obtuse, obdurate, recalcitrant men who at first are unperceptive of Jesus' messiahship, then oppose its style and character, and finally totally reject it. As the coup de grace, Mark closes his Gospel without rehabilitating the disciples.[5]

Werner H. Kelber offers an example of a more moderate negative view of the disciples. He entitles the second chapter of *Mark's Story of Jesus*, "The Blindness of the Disciples." Kelber makes a sharp conclusion about the character of the disciples:

> It is the disciples (and not the Jews!) who in this section [4:35-8:21] have emerged as the true opponents of Jesus. Their failure is epitomized in the concluding trip back [from the Gentile side of the lake] to the Jewish side. The hardness of heart accusation, together with that of an entire lack of perception, reverses the disciples' earlier privileged insider status. They have failed to grasp the logic of Jesus' journey and are about to be an obstacle

on the way to the Kingdom. The insiders have become opponents and outsiders.[6]

When Kelber discusses the experience of Jesus and his disciples during a storm at sea (4:35-41), the disciples are presented as panic-stricken by the storm, frightened by Jesus' rebuke, and ignorant concerning Jesus' identity.[7]

While Kelber describes the disciples as being blind, another alternative is to interpret the disciples as being both present and absent to Jesus. The disciples are in the boat with Jesus because Jesus has instructed them to go to the other side of the sea. The disciples find themselves in the storm because they have been with Jesus in obedience. That they panic and awaken Jesus to challenge his concern for their lives is indicative of their simultaneous absence to Jesus. They were both with Jesus and not with Jesus. They have been obedient, but they are now faithless.

The experience of the disciples being both with Jesus and not with Jesus is further explicated in Mark's feeding story in 6:30-44. Having sought solitude from the demands of their ministry, Jesus and his disciples find themselves met by a crowd of people whom Jesus decides to teach. As the day grows on, the disciples suggest dismissing the assembly in order for the crowd to buy food and eat. When Jesus instructs his disciples to feed the people, the disciples confess their inadequacy to provide sufficient food for the overwhelming crowd. Jesus instructs the disciples to bring him what they can find. Having secured five loaves of bread and two fish, the disciples are instructed to organize the crowd into groups and feed the people with food Jesus has multiplied. All the people are fed, and twelve full baskets are left.

Here the disciples are present to Jesus in ministry through taking leadership to organize and feed the multitude, then they are absent to Jesus in their lack of compassion to the level shown by Jesus. They cannot fathom how they can manage to feed the vast multitude of people, yet they obey Jesus' instructions to bring the food they can find. This is an example of how the disciples are simultaneously present and absent to Jesus.

When Jesus responds to criticism of his disciples by scribes and Pharisees who are offended that the disciples eat without washing their hands (7:1ff.), Jesus proceeds to expose the hypocrisy of those who honor God with words but without deeds. Following Jesus' instruction to the people that what one takes in does not defile, but that which comes from within, the disciples are confused and ask Jesus what he means. Jesus further explains, but he also responds, "are you also without understanding?" (7:18). Again the disciples are present to Jesus but, in their confusion, they are absent to him.

One further example of the simultaneous presence and absence of Jesus' disciples occurs in 10:35-45. Previously, Jesus has informed his disciples that they are approaching Jerusalem, where he will be arrested, condemned, given to the Gentiles, humiliated, killed, and risen. After Jesus tells the disciples of his coming experiences, James and John—two of Jesus' first four disciples—are portrayed as lobbying for seats of honor when Jesus comes into his glory. Jesus must inform them that they are unaware of what they are asking. The cup from which Jesus drinks is bitter, and they would drink from that cup and share in his baptism. He then goes on to teach the disciples that authority over one another is antithetical to the character of his disciples. Instead, honor among disciples comes through selfless servanthood patterned after the Son of man having given his life as a ransom for many. Once again, the disciples are present to Jesus as he moves toward his destiny, yet they are absent to Jesus in terms of comprehending the true nature of discipleship.

Mark's treatment of the disciples prior to the passion-resurrection narrative shows two dimensions of their relationship to Jesus. Initially, the disciples are loyal followers who appear to be with Jesus in every way. Subsequently, they appear to be with Jesus, but not quite with Jesus. This pattern, however, is not sequential. The references used above show an overlap of the presence and presence/absence motifs in the flow of Mark's story. This is an important quality. The presence and absence of the disciples in relationship to Jesus is not neatly defined in chronological order. There is an ebb and flow of the relationship which seems to drift increasingly toward the simultaneous presence and absence of the disciples. As Mark's story continues toward the passion and resurrection, the question of relationship between Jesus and his disciples intensifies. The question of God's presence also looms in the background. We turn now to the intensity of the passion-resurrection narrative found in Mark 14:1-16:8.[8]

ABSENCE AND PRESENCE
IN MARK'S PASSION-RESURRECTION NARRATIVE

Early in Mark the disciples are loyal followers of Jesus. As the story progresses, we see that the disciples are with Jesus, but they are not quite with Jesus. According to Weeden,

> The crucifixion story, both on the level of narrative and in the history of the struggle of theological traditions in the M[ar]kan community, dramatizes the mysterious paradox of authentic Christian existence: "Power (life) is made perfect in weakness" (2 Cor. 12:9).[9]

For our purposes, "the mysterious paradox of authentic Christian existence" includes the concept that God is both absent and present to humanity.

Mark's portrait of Jesus shows that the most significant relationships in the life of Jesus are his relationship with God and his relationship with his disciples. Attending to the narrative's treatment of Jesus' secondary relationship with his disciples may illuminate an appreciation for Jesus' primary relationship with God. The experience of the disciples' relationship to Jesus can be understood as a paradigm of Jesus' experience of God's relationship to him. Suggesting this paradigm does not imply an absolute correspondence in the relationships at every point, but important parallels may be present in Jesus' experience of these two critical relationships.

I am not suggesting that the disciples' behavior toward Jesus is an identical parallel to God's behavior toward Jesus. Reading the relationship of the disciples to Jesus paradigmatically in relationship to God's relationship to Jesus extends only to the point of suggesting how Jesus perceived his relationship with God during his passion. Consequently, when one reads that Jesus was abandoned by the twelve, the paradigmatic application does not require one to conclude that Jesus was abandoned by God in the same way. The abandonment by the disciples does suggest, however, that Jesus' experience with God during this time was a legitimate experience of abandonment from his perspective. One's experience of something can be real even when another reality is extant.

This paradigm is applicable to the categories of presence, presence and absence, and absence experienced by Jesus. Observing that Jesus' disciples were absent to Jesus can be seen as a paradigm of God's absence to Jesus from Jesus' perspective. This suggestion, however, only speaks to Jesus' perception of the absence of God. It does not speak to God's abandonment. We cannot propose conclusions concerning this concept from God's perspective with any degree of probability. Even turning to the concept of a trinitarian interruption in the life of God for the sake of the world does not necessitate the conceptualization that God has departed from Jesus. Furthermore, the holism inherent in African-American philosophical and theological conceptualizations and confidence in God's faithfulness make concluding that God would actually depart from Jesus inconceivable.

The relationship of the disciples to Jesus can be understood as paradigmatic of the relationship between Jesus and God. Prior to the passion-resurrection narrative, there has been a movement from a sense of presence to simultaneous presence and absence. In the passion-resurrection narrative, the movement continues.

Presence and Absence

After informing the reader about the plotting of the chief priests and scribes to kill Jesus near the time of the Passover and the Feast of Unleavened Bread (14:1-2), Mark tells the story of a woman offering a surprising display of love to Jesus (14:3-9). She shatters a flask of expensive ointment and pours it over Jesus' head. Her presence to Jesus is indicated by her extravagant expression of anointing Jesus with a "mysterious, extremely expensive, and pure" ointment.[10] The disciples are offended at this display of extravagance and criticize her "wastefulness." To their surprise, Jesus reprimands their response and commends the act of the woman. She is willing do to what they are unwilling to do: she expresses committed love for Jesus. Immediately following this event, Judas goes to the chief priests to collaborate on a treacherous plan for Jesus' murder (14:10-11). This is an intriguing portrayal of the absence of the twelve disciples to Jesus simultaneous to the presence of one disciple.

The juxtaposition of the presence and absence of the disciples of Jesus is further seen in their profession of committed faithfulness and their abysmal demonstration of unfaithfulness. After Jesus and the twelve share in the passover meal and enter the Mount of Olives, he tells the twelve of their forthcoming scattering and informs them that he will be raised up after the crucifixion and will go before them to Galilee. Peter promises his undying loyalty to Jesus, regardless of the actions of the others, to which Jesus predicts Peter's betrayal. The remainder of the twelve commit themselves to absolute loyalty—even unto death (14:26-31). In Kim E. Dewey's perspective,

> In 14:26-31 the denial theme is linked to the overriding theme of the falling away (scandal) of the disciples. Jesus prophesies that they will be scandalized and, when Peter protests, he predicts precisely how Peter will fulfill the prophecy (i.e., by denial). The movement of this story is toward the prophecy of the denial.[11]

This passage is a picture of conflicting prophecies. Jesus prophesies denial; Peter prophesies devotion. Perhaps this portrays "an illustration of the fundamental gulf between God and man."[12] The presence yet absence of the disciples looms large in this portrait of contrasting predictions. To the disciples' profession of loyalty, Jesus predicts the ultimate reversal.

Another portrait of the absence and presence of the disciples to Jesus is in the Gethsemane scene (14:32-42). While Jesus instructs the majority of the twelve to sit while he prays, he takes with him Peter, James, and John. Jesus has a more intimate relationship with these disciples. The agony of Jesus' crucifixion intensifies as he confesses his sorrow and shows his distress. He asks the three to watch with him while he prays, but Jesus goes on further, to pray alone. When Jesus returns to find the three asleep, he addresses Peter with a rebuke to their unfaithfulness and a charge to faithfulness. Peter was not alone in failing Jesus, but "Simon Peter represents the entire group of disciples."[13] All the disciples had pledged loyalty unto death, but they cannot even remain awake for awhile with Jesus in his agony. Jesus returns two additional times to find them sleeping. "The loneliness of the Son of Man is accented by the fact that while he struggles in prayer he is surrounded by men who do not understand him, but fall asleep."[14]

As the story progresses, it is clear that Jesus will face the bitterness of his crucifixion alone. While both present and absent to Jesus, the disciples are becoming increasingly absent.

The Prominence of Absence

That Jesus' disciples are absent to him is clear at the account of his arrest (14:43-52). First Judas identifies Jesus to the arresters by kissing him. That Judas was one of the twelve "accentuates the grievousness of Jesus' fate. Even those closest to him have not understood him."[15] Then Jesus' disciples "all forsook him, and fled" (14:50). Jesus is now completely isolated from the twelve. Those who had earlier pledged unfailing loyalty have now left Jesus to face the bitterness of the coming events alone.

Jesus' isolation from the disciples is further highlighted by Peter's denial (14:66-72). When asked about his identity as an associate of the arrested Jesus, Peter denies his acquaintance with Jesus three times. The irony of this denial is that Peter is not called on to defend his discipleship to a hostile crowd or in a formal debate with enemies of Jesus. Peter's opportunity to demonstrate his promised loyalty is before a servant girl and a small group of people. He need only admit that he knows Jesus. Peter's pathetic performance fulfills the prophecy of Jesus. Although Peter realizes this and weeps, he does not recant his denial.

Jesus is completely abandoned by his disciples in Mark 15. There is no mention of the disciples during the accounts of Jesus' interrogation before Pilate (15:1-15), the soldiers' taunting behavior toward Jesus (15:16-20), the crucifixion event (15:21-32), the death scene (15:33-41), or the burial (15:42-47). The disciples are conspicuously absent. In fact, after Peter's dismal disavowal of discipleship, there is no mention of the twelve male disciples throughout the remainder of the narrative. Those to whom Jesus had been closest were now furthest removed from him. Jesus had not moved away from them; he had stayed his course. The disciples were absent. They had abandoned Jesus.

Fortunately, the twelve were not the exclusive followers of Jesus. As the story unfolds, Jesus is alone throughout his appearance before Pilate, his humiliation by the soldiers, and his crucifixion. However, there are other disciples who appear, and while the twelve are a paradigm of God's absence, the emerging disciples can be considered a paradigm for God's presence.

The Prominence of Presence

While the closeness of the twelve disciples to Jesus diminishes, new disciples appear. The emerging disciples are women who have followed Jesus. Despite the fact that the women disciples are looking upon the crucifixion from a distance, they have not abandoned Jesus, as did the twelve men.

Not only are the women disciples present at the crucifixion, they are present at the burial.[16] They are the disciples who are present to Jesus to the end. As the narrative continues, the women are also the first and only disciples who visit the tomb after the sabbath (16:1-2).

Mark's portrayal of women in relation to Jesus is significant. The passion-resurrection narrative begins and ends with a juxtaposition of the ministry of women disciples with the abandonment of the twelve men. A woman anoints Jesus' body in preparation for burial in 14:8, and women come to the tomb with the same intention in 16:1.

> The implication is plain. The consistent faithfulness of the women in their identification with the crucified Christ (cf. also 15:40-41) contrasts with the almost consistent faithlessness of Peter and the twelve.[17]

Yet their presence is tempered by uncertainty at the command of the young man they meet at the empty tomb.

Absence and Presence in the Passion-Resurrection Narrative

Andrew T. Lincoln concludes that Mark's presentation of the disciples—male and female—is negative. While the reader expects the women to leave the tomb with joy, the reader is surprised at the failure of the women in light of the resurrection (16:7-8). The effect of this interpretation is that hearers and readers of Mark, both original and contemporary, recognized a stark realism in the story. However, the story did not end with the ending of Mark.

> It continued into the time of the readers. The effectiveness of its final juxtaposition of promise and failure within the context of the Gospel's narrative world depended on the belief that the one

outstanding promise about the parousia of the Son of man would soon be fulfilled.[18]

Gerald O'Collins, S. J., offers three clear alternatives for interpreting the women's response at Mark's conclusion. First, they may be afraid of humans or they may fear God. Second, their silence may be taken to be disobedience to the young man's instructions, or they may stand in awe of their received revelation. Third, is their flight parallel to that of 14:50, or is it from terror of divine intervention? O'Collins argues that it is erroneous to equate the negative view of the male disciples to the female disciples because, rather than being consistently portrayed as unfaithful, the women are consistently seen as good.[19] That the women are silent is consistent with Mark's earlier emphasis on people's astonishment and amazement at Jesus' teaching (1:22) and power over unclean spirits (1:27). Consequently,

> Faced with the uniquely great revelation of God in the resurrection of the crucified Jesus, the silent and fearful flight of the women is not only understandable but also highly appropriate.[20]

Arland J. Hultgren concurs.

> It is more likely that Mark intends to portray the women as overcome by awe at what has taken place—a *mysterium tremendum*—when he describes them as trembling, astonished and fearful.[21]

A contrary perspective is that the fear in the women is reasonable but their silence is disobedient to the young man's instructions. Contrary to those earlier in Mark who had been instructed to silence (e.g., 1:44; 7:46) but professed their good news, these who are charged to tell the good news are silent.

Regardless of whether one concludes that the women were disobedient or understandably astonished, the women disciples appear both present and absent. Reading the relationship of the women disciples to Jesus as a paradigm indicative of Jesus' experience of God's relationship to him implies that one can interpret Jesus' experience of God as presence and absence to him at the crucifixion. This interpretation is consistent with the conclusion of Chapter Three, where analyses of antebellum African-American spirituals that focus on suffering and the crucifixion indicate that amid the extremities of abject human suffering, God is experienced as both present and absent. This is how God was to Jesus at the crucifixion. This is how God is with humanity in the extremities of human suffering.

According to Jesus' predictions, the larger experience of his resurrection was certain (8:31; 9:31; 10:34).[22] Correspondingly, the larger reality for Christians is that while God is sometimes present and sometimes absent to us (from our perspectives), the larger context is that God is ever present with us. One's current experiences of the extremities of human suffering may overcome the capacity to affirm this concept at given moments of calamity. Nonetheless, this reading of Mark's gospel points toward the hope of God's presence in the midst of God's apparent absence.

INTERPRETING JESUS' CRY OF DERELICTION

The relationship of the disciples to Jesus can be articulated in the following terms: 1) presence; 2) absence; and 3) presence and absence. The final portrait of the relationship is an ambiguity of presence and absence seen in the women disciples at the empty tomb. They are faithfully present to Jesus, but they are fearful and silent in response to the empty tomb and their instructions to proclaim the resurrection. The relationship of the disciples to Jesus may be construed as paradigmatic of God's relationship to Jesus. That God is sometimes clearly present, other times present and absent, and still at other times apparently absent is critical to our consideration of Jesus' cry of dereliction. The conceptualization of God's relationship to Jesus in this way is consistent with our earlier theological articulation of the antebellum African-American understanding of Godforsakenness. However, this concept is not universally accepted.

The Cry and Psalm 22

Jesus' cry is a quotation of the first line of Psalm 22. As a whole, the psalm consists of lament, prayer, and praise. The lament is reflective of a contradiction between theology and experience. The theology born of tradition and the past experience of Israel affirms trust in God.

However, the experience of the lamenter is diametrically opposed to the theology.

> The God of covenant, who was believed not to have deserted his faithful people, appeared to have forsaken this worshipper who, in sickness, faced the door of death. And it was the sense of being forsaken by God that was the fundamental problem—more grave than the actual condition of sickness and the threat of death.[23]

Modern interpretations of Jesus' cry generally follow two paths. One view attends to his prayerful trust, while the other focuses on his desolation.[24]

A Triumphant Prayer?

Some have contended that 15:34 is not a cry of agony but a cry of power, triumph, and judgment. Weeden cites Johannes Schreiber's interpretation of Jesus' cry as one of triumph. Schreiber sees Jesus' death in Mark in terms of Old Testament Jewish apocalypticism. Hence Jesus' cry of dereliction is interpreted as the "triumphant moment in the narrative."[25] Carroll Stuhlmueller contends that Israel implicitly accepts what is explicitly denied in Psalm 22—that God "who is said to have abandoned his people" is near them, concerned for them, and hears their cries.[26]

Boomershine argues that "the implication is that Jesus sang this lament of David."[27] Singing the song of a righteous sufferer feeling the abandonment of God does not imply Jesus had lost his faith. To the contrary, this argument holds, Jesus demonstrated his faith inasmuch as he "recites a traditional prayer of a righteous Jew who is near death."[28]

John Paul Heil argues that Jesus' quotation of the first line of Psalm 22 is a plea for the "why" of his passion.

> Although indicative of his anguish as he dies alone and without divine intervention, Jesus' loud scream is not a cry of despair but the lamentful prayer of the suffering just one, uttered with total trust in his God. Instead of coming down from the cross and saving himself as his taunters propose (15,29-32), Jesus, with

confidence in God's sovereign plan, addresses him twice as "my God," calling for God to disclose the purpose "why" he has abandoned him to death.[29]

Psalm 22 belongs to a genre of personal laments in the psalter that speak to the experience of forsakenness by the righteous. God is begged not to abandon ultimately (Pss. 27:9; 38:21; 119:8), God is begged to remember (Pss. 13:1; 74:19), God is asked why God has forgotten, cast off, and hidden Godself from the petitioner.[30] Kenneth Grayston contends that the suffering of these references is really attributed to the enemies of the righteous.

> Indeed, these complaints are not to be read naively as statements of theological fact; they are a form of pleading, intended to provoke a reassuring response from God. . . . When, therefore, Jesus uttered the loud cry from Ps 22:1 he was following a central tradition that affirms not that God is absent from the sufferer but that he [sic] is present and open to entreaty.[31]

While some interpret Jesus' quotation from Psalm 22 as trusting prayer, this approach is not the only option available.

A Tragic Cry

Some have suggested that Jesus' quotation of the first line of the psalm refers to the psalm in its entirety. Thus Jesus' cry is that of suffering in anticipation of God's vindication. However, Joel B. Green concludes that this approach intends to remove an alleged offensive connotation of the cry for primitive Christianity. The effort fails for two reasons. First, the use of psalms in this way is substantially later than Mark's composition. Second, there is little evidence indicating that one verse could suggest a reference to the Old Testament passage in which the verse was contained while ignoring its own meaning.[32]

Mary Ann Tolbert shows that the narrative to this point has led the audience to conceive that God loves Jesus as God's own son and that God is faithful to people of faith. Since God has been portrayed as such, one could argue that Jesus must be wrong, but the narrative has shown Jesus never to be wrong. Tolbert contends that the solution to the perplexing dilemma is found in the form of Jesus' cry. Jesus cries to the one who has allegedly abandoned him for the reason for the abandonment. Jesus prays to the God who supposedly has left him.

> The irony created by the conflict of form and content in Jesus' cry to God moves very close to paradox, in which two contradictory positions are both held to be true. Jesus is forsaken by God, and at the same time God is available to be called upon.[33]

Jesus' cry lucidly indicates a sense of abandonment. "His passion and death are portrayed as moments of his being abandoned by his disciples and even—from the standpoint of the dying Jesus—by God."[34] Alister McGrath poignantly articulates the situation with this text. "Either God is not present at all in this situation, or else he is present in a remarkable and paradoxical way."[35] Failing to consider the cry of Jesus as a tragic expression of his experience of forsakenness can be devastating. As C. S. Mann explains:

> to erode in any way the humanity of Jesus is to be on the way to producing a docetic Jesus (against which the fourth gospel and the Johannine letters wax vehemently) and making of Jesus a man of certitude and not of faith, far removed from that humanity of ours which Christian faith says he shared.[36]

With the exception of 15:34, Jesus always addressed God as *Abba* in his prayers. Nowhere else in Judaism is this address to God found. That Jesus addressed God as *Abba* indicates the unique relationship between God and Jesus. Joachim Jeremias contends that the only reason for the exceptional address here is because of the nature of its being a quotation.[37]

The interpretation of 15:34 which holds

> that Jesus, as a substitute for sinners, was forsaken by the Father, is inconsistent with the love of God and the oneness of purpose with the Father manifest in the atoning ministry of Jesus.[38]

Vincent Taylor goes on to claim that understanding Jesus' cry of forsakenness as a final expression of faith in reference to Psalm 22 in its entirety is a reactionary response on the part of those who fail to see the solemnity of the cry.

The depths of the saying are too deep to be plumbed, but the least inadequate interpretations are those which find in it a sense of desolation in which Jesus felt the horror of sin so deeply that for a time the closeness of his communion with the Father was obscured.[39]

Schweizer concisely summarizes the point.

This cry clings to the fact that God is real at all times, even in those times when neither experience nor thought can lay hold of him. It is not a question here of whether or not Jesus uttered this saying, or even the sayings handed down by Luke and John. It makes no difference whether he said any part of it or none of it. This passage presents the search for a faith which knows that God is real even in times when the believer feels forsaken and when the resources of thinking and experience have been exhausted.[40]

When Mark's narrative reports Jesus' cry of dereliction, "My God, my God, why hast thou forsaken me?" Jesus can be understood as articulating his experience of God's absence from him. His experience was real. It must be noted, however, that Jesus' articulation of his experience of Godforsakenness is from his perspective. One can further interpret that there was a concurrent supcrareality. That is, God was present, even in the midst of Jesus' experience of God's absence. As Elizabeth A. Johnson notes: "Although for a time there was no glimmer of hope, God was near at hand, nevertheless, and Jesus was not ultimately abandoned."[41]

SUMMARY

The relationship of God to Jesus, from Jesus' perspective, can be understood paradigmatically by observing the relationship of Jesus' disciples to Jesus. We can see a movement from the prominence of presence, to the presence and absence of the disciples to Jesus, through a prominence of absence. At the end, we can see the model of simultaneous presence and absence in the disciples. Construing these paradigms as possibly indicative of God's relationship to Jesus, this framework can be used to interpret Jesus' cry of forsakenness as meaning that God was absent to Jesus, from Jesus' perspective, but actually present. God's presence is certain in spite of one's experience of God's absence. Perhaps God's presence can be known through or in one's experience of absence.

CHAPTER FIVE

Implications for Contemporary Theology

Significant strides were made by African Americans in the years subsequent to the Emancipation Proclamation. W. H. Council reported the following statistics about the American Negro in 1901: the illiteracy rate had been reduced 45 percent in 35 years, 1.5 million children attended common school, and 40,000 students were engaged in higher education. There were 30,000 negro teachers, 20,000 students in trade school, 1,200 students in scientific programs, 1,000 students in business courses, and 17,000 students had graduated from educational programs. Negro libraries held 250,000 volumes. There were 156 institutions of higher learning, 500 doctors, 300 books authored, 250 lawyers, 3 banks, 3 magazines, and 400 newspapers. The value of black libraries was $500,000. There was $12 million in school properties, $37 million in church property, 230,000 farms valued at $400 million, 150,000 homes (aside from farm homes) valued at $325 million, personal property worth $325 million, and American negroes raised $10 million for their own education.[1] All this progress was made in less than 40 years following the abolition of slavery.

A century following the Emancipation Proclamation, however, there was only modest advancement for a minimum number of black Americans. One hundred years subsequent to the signing of the monumental document, black Americans still found an absence of opportunity. As Martin Luther King, Jr., said:

As the then Vice-President, Lyndon B. Johnson, phrased it: "Emancipation was a Proclamation but not a fact." The pen of the Great Emancipator had moved the Negro into the sunlight of physical freedom, but actual conditions had left him behind in the shadow of political, psychological, social, economic and intellectual bondage.[2]

Those who led the Civil Rights Movement intended a result of their efforts to be freedom's sunlight penetrating the shadows of bondage and unraveling the tangled web of oppression that obstructed the progress of African-American people and, consequently, the country. This vision has not been realized for the masses. One manifestation of this unrealized goal is the abject poverty in which most African-American children live. Marian Wright Edelman notes that compared to white children, black children are twice as likely to live in substandard housing, be unemployed as teenagers, and have no parent employed. Black children are three times more likely than white children to be poor. Black children are five times more likely than white children to be dependent on welfare.[3] While the causes of these unnerving realities are varied, in many cases the result is extreme human suffering. Undoubtedly the suffering encountered by the children and their families is, at times, virtually or actually unbearable.

CRITICAL REFLECTIONS

It can be argued that human suffering is normative rather than aberrational. Globally, people must live under the harshness of racism, classism, and sexism. Black North Americans, like the majority of the world's peoples, suffer under some or all of these forms of oppressive systems. However, rather than acquiescence to oppression, there exists a yearning for physical freedom, spiritual empowerment, and cultural liberation.[4]

The dominant influence upon the religious development of Africans and African Americans has been the struggle for meaningful existence, and suffering is integral to this struggle.[5] Suffering is a transcendental cultural reality not limited to oppressed peoples of particular ethnic, class, or gender groups, but transcending these classifications to embrace the entirety of humanity. However, African Americans encounter human suffering in two particular ways. First, black people share the suffering that is common to all of humanity—illness, broken relationships, death, accidents, wars, and the like. Second, black suffering has been experienced because of slavery, discrimination, and racism. "This sociological grid of blacks provides a solidarity that transcends even

membership in the Christian religion."[6] An interpretation of Jesus' cry
of forsakenness is needed from the perspective of people who have
suffered and continue to suffer greatly.

African-American Christian ideas of God have developed differently than most ideas born of Eurocentric theologians. "Modern theologians," according to Ronald Thiemann, "seek to assert God's prior
reality in an intellectual and cultural atmosphere in which that reality
is no longer assumed."[7] While Thiemann's comment addresses the
crisis of revelation caused by the challenges of atheism and pluralism,
the principle holds in relation to African-American perspectives as
well. African-American Christians have not known God through God's
revealed word alone, and the idea of God among black Christians is
made problematic because of their history of victimization and despoil-
ment. "The idea of God for African-Americans is rooted in the concrete
realities of their experiences."[8] Consequently, contextualization is
crucial to theology in African-American perspective.

Contextualization is integral to postcolonial-era contemporary theology. The Christian church no longer accepts *in toto* theology developed in the North Atlantic theological community. J. Deotis Roberts
asserts that theology

> needs to be developed in context. . . . The time has come for all
> who participate in theological reflection—whether in Europe or
> the Americas, black, feminist, and Hispanic—to allow theologi-
> ans . . . to do their own theological reflection.[9]

Roberts' appeal for contextual method in theology intends to con-
tribute to mutual understanding, cultivate increasing theological depth,
and facilitate the process of spiritual maturation.

Antebellum life is critical for an appreciation of contemporary
North American life. Historian and novelist Shelby Foote argues that
critical examination of the Civil War is an "absolute prerequisite" for
understanding America today, since the Civil War and the issues
surrounding it are definitive for the historical development of the
United States.[10] George P. Rawick offers similar insight. "Black history in the United States must be viewed as an integral, if usually
antagonistic, part of the history of the American people."[11] James H.
Cone contends that "one's social and historical context decides not only
the questions we address to God but also the mode or form of the

answers given to the questions."[12] Given the historical perspectives of Foote and Rawick, and in light of Cone's contention that theological issues are historically contextualized, one can affirm that what is true for history is likewise applicable for theology. It would seem, then, that North American theology could benefit from greater attention to the Civil War era and its related issues because theology evolves in relationship to its historical context. Studying antebellum African-American life offers promise for theological investigation and reflection.

PATHS TO PURSUE

What, if any, are the implications of our conclusions for contemporary theology?

Possibilities for Contemporary African Americans

Humanity in general and African Americans in particular encounter experiences of extreme human suffering. Contemporary youth, for example, endure unfathomable encounters with violence, pregnancy, and crime. The National Education Association and the National School Board Association report the following:

> 100,000 American children will go to school carrying a gun. ... More than 40 children are killed or injured by a firearm every school day. . . . 39 percent of urban school districts had a shooting or knifing last year. . . . 15 percent of schools use metal detectors.[13]

Planned Parenthood offers these statistics:

> Every year more than 1 million U. S. teenagers become pregnant. . . . U. S. teenagers have one of the highest pregnancy rates in the Western world, double the rates in England, France and Canada. . . . 73 percent of births to teens result from unintended pregnancies; 4 in 10 teen pregnancies end in abortion.[14]

The 1992 F.B.I. Uniform Crime Report from the United States Department of Justice indicates grim facts:

Juvenile offenders spend an average of 265 days in long-term correction facilities, according to a 1991 report. . . . 194,137 people under 18 were arrested for violent crimes in 1992; 2,343 of those were charged with murder. . . . In 1992, 2,428 juveniles were murdered. . . . From 1965 to 1990, the overall murder arrest rate for juveniles soared 332 percent.[15]

The physical and social isolation of poor black communities result in the exacerbation of certain experiences of extreme human suffering and tragedy. African-American teenagers and young adults who are in communities of the dependent poor or underclass face continual escalating crises. Black teenage females have one of the highest pregnancy rates in the world, and black males have the highest homicide and imprisonment rates in the United States. While debates continue concerning the fundamental causes of these crises, one might ask "Where is God?" in the midst of this human suffering.

If one can read the relationship of Jesus' disciples to him paradigmatically as pointing toward Jesus' experience of God's relationship to him, one can infer that African-American women disciples can be understood as a paradigm of God's presence in the apparent experience of absence known to many other African Americans.

Females are the predominant constituency of African-American mainline denominations.[16] The dominance of female membership in congregations, however, has not translated proportionately into recognized leadership. The black church's progress has depended heavily on the support of women, but women have not been afforded equitable opportunities for guidance in churches. C. Eric Lincoln and Lawrence H. Mamiya contend that "Both historical and contemporary evidence underscore the fact that black churches could scarcely have survived without the active support of black women."[17]

While many aspects of African-American life seem characterized by an existence that can be described as Godforsakenness, the presence of African-American women and their record of faithful support and endurance can be construed as paradigmatic of the larger reality of God's presence with the abandoned of life, in spite of God's apparent absence from the perspective of the suffering. While suffering African-American people may experience God's absence, God can be presumed present as one views the faithful presence of African-American female disciples paradigmatically as God's faithful presence to God's own.

Possibilities beyond the Markan Narrative

This study has proposed an understanding of Godforsakenness that holds that God can be presumed present in the midst of the apparent simultaneity of God's presence and absence as well as in one's experience of God's absence. This concept holds possibilities for interpreting God's relationship to Israel while enslaved in Egypt.

While God can be understood in Exodus as the transcendent and sovereign Lord who acts with unqualified authority, Terence E. Fretheim suggests that the Exodus story contains suffering metaphors for God that qualify the sovereignty metaphors. When divine sovereignty interacts with human agency, suffering metaphors of God evolve. For example, God's intervention on behalf of the Hebrews (3:7-10) evolves from God's encounter with human suffering (2:24-25). Further, when God seems to be absent in the story, God may be conceived as being present through the activity of human agents (e.g., the midwives [1:15-22] and Pharaoh's daughter [2:5-11]).[18]

In Exodus 3, God reveals to Moses God's name—Yahweh. While God's hiddenness may be construed in this revelation, Ee Kon Kim suggests a paradoxical understanding of God acting on behalf of the Hebrews as well as hiding from them in the giving of the name Yahweh. Further, one exegetically discovers that the revelation of God in the burning bush event occurs within the narrative of the people's oppression. Hence one can infer that the unconsumed burning bush symbolizes that the oppressed will survive their oppression. Kim concludes that God's name does not hide God's identity but has a theological function and contextual connotation that understands God's name to mean, "I am the one who causes compassion." Yahweh is seen as existing and acting from within the context of the politically, economically, and socially oppressed.[19]

One can see that this possesses possibilities for explication in reference to the story of the enslaved Hebrews. There is additional potential for the use of the methodology in considering the concept of God's presumed presence in the midst of the apparent absence of God in human suffering for peoples of the Two-Thirds World—Africa, Asia, Latin America, and the Middle East—who live in closer proximity to political oppression and the subhuman conditions of hunger, homelessness, and disease than do people in the West.[20]

Possibilities for Other Social Contexts

This methodology is not confined to the context of African-American theology. Its applicability is potentially viable for other oppressed communities.

Many Latin Americans live under economic oppression related to the economic policies of the United States government. The debt level of many Latin American countries leads to the dismantling of health and educational systems in order to make payments on international debt. With the majority of Latin American workers earning minimum wages, the resultant consequences include poverty and oppression. Theology in many quarters of Latin America and other impoverished communities has taken on liberation as a core component. This is true for Roman Catholicism as well as Protestant evangelicalism.[21]

Gustavo Gutiérrez suggests that there is but one way to discover words with which to talk about God amid

the starvation of millions, the humiliation of races regarded as inferior, discrimination against women (especially women who are poor), systematic social injustice, terrorism of every kind, and the corpse filled groves of Peru's Ayachucho.[22]

Gutiérrez contends that the way to deal with the question of God in relationship to the suffering of the innocent is to do so from personal involvement with the suffering poor. When the suffering of the innocent is considered alongside the mystery of the cross, one can do theology that is relevant rather than whimsical, and one can speak of hope in God's presence and activity with the innocent suffering because of one's engagement with their suffering. Hence Latin American liberation theology and liberation theologies of other contexts identify Jesus with the poor and perceive Jesus to help people recover their human dignity. God is perceived as being revealed as God of the poor, and God is with the poor in the midst of their oppression.

More than a decade ago, Adrio König noted from his Southern African perspective that some forms of liberation theology were one-sided. According to König, liberation theology, while posturing itself as a theology of protest, was sometimes accused of failing to adequately address the equally essential correlative concept of the theology of comfort. The argument follows that in spite of calls to recognize and resist political suffering, as well as the movement to restructure political systems in favor of the oppressed and victimized, liberation theology should offer comfort to those who will continue to endure suffering. König does not seek to place the theology of comfort above liberation theology; rather he seeks to establish the theology of comfort as an essential correlate to liberation theology. König argues that "the gospel is more than a protest against suffering. It is also a message of comfort for people whose suffering will at least for a time endure."[23]

Finally, Sun Ai Lee Park's observations about the presence of God in the midst of the suffering of oppressed people is in harmony with the direction and further applicability of this study. She argues:

> the God of the oppressed people as God has been revealed in the liberation of the Israelites in the Egyptian bondage, in which were revealed the principles of God's involvement in human history and affirming the same principles through prophetic tradition and completed in the event of Jesus Christ demonstrates God's presence in a completely open way.

> Urban industrial missioners see God in the factory; various people who are engaged in struggles for dignified survival see God's presence in the midst of their struggles.[24]

This study is a theological investigation into the doctrine of God. It seeks a response to the question concerning where God is when the atrocities of human experience are beyond comprehension. Answering the question "Where is God?" is to move toward comprehension of the core of the nature of God's being. The penetrating edge of the question "Why has God forsaken me?" implies a presumption of the abandonment of God. To correctly respond to this piercing inquiry is to propose a foundational conceptualization concerning the whole of theology.

My proposed answer to the explicit question of the dying Jesus of Nazareth and the implicit question of enslaved African Americans in the antebellum era is that God was present. To conclude that God was present, even though apparently absent from the perspective of the suffering ones, is to propose that God was, and is, the One who is absolutely faithful. That God's manifestation to humanity may not always be consistent from our point of view is not to infer that God is not faithful. Apparent inconsistency is not equivalent to actual unfaithfulness. Stated differently, apparent consistency does not equate to actual fidelity.

Based on the narratives examined in this study and the theological analysis of spirituals, the accurate conclusion to draw from the theology of the slaves is that God was presumed to be the one who never abandons, even in the midst of extremities when suffering exceeds the boundaries of intelligibility. When suffering is inexplicable, indescribable, unbearable, God does not abandon. One can seek to ground one's concept of God on traditional articulations of ideas such as omniscience, omnipotence, and the like. A foundational understanding about the nature of God is that God is understood as the One who is always present. When one listens to the stories of the experiences of antebellum African-American life and hears the theology of spirituals that sing of suffering and the crucifixion, one may reasonably conclude that, for those who belong to God and experience the extremities of human suffering, God is with us.

Notes

1. NARRATIVE AND AFRICAN-AMERICAN THEOLOGY

1. Harold Scheub, *African Images* (New York: McGraw-Hill, 1972), p. v.

2. Michelle Cliff, " 'I Found God in Myself and I Loved Her/I Loved Her Fiercely': More Thoughts on the Work of Black Women Artists," *Journal of Feminist Studies in Religion* 1 (1986): 16.

3. Nicholas C. Cooper-Lewter and Henry H. Mitchel, *Soul Theology: The Heart of American Black Culture* (New York: Harper & Row, 1986), p. 8.

4. Lawrence W. Levine, *Black Culture and Black Consciousness: Afro-American Folk Thought from Slavery to Freedom* (New York: Oxford University Press, 1977), p. 97.

5. Ibid., p. 102. Slaveholders often believed that slave tales were children's stories told by childlike minds. Members of the slaveholding community did not realize that they were often the object of ridicule in the animal trickster tales.

6. Ibid., p. 107.

7. Charles Joyner, "The Trickster and the Fool: Folktales and Identity among Southern Plantation Slaves," *Plantation Society* 2 (1986): 149-156.

8. Othal Hawthorne Lakey, *The Rise of Colored Methodism* (Dallas, TX: Crescendo Book Publications, 1972), shows how slaveholders misused the Bible to teach inferiority and submission. William Capers' catechism taught that God made slaves from the dust of the ground, God expected humility from slaves, God required love with the totality of one's being, and the servants' duty to masters or mistresses was: "To serve them with a good will heartily and not with eye-service" (p. 38).

9. See Anthony C. Thiselton, *New Horizons in Hermeneutics: The Theory and Practice of Transforming Biblical Reading* (Grand Rapids, MI: Zondervan Publishing House, 1992).

10. I elect to use the term *Two-Thirds World* as opposed to Third World because of its more positive connotation and more accurate description of the people to whom the term refers. Further, growing numbers of people in these underdeveloped and developing countries are defining themselves in this way.

11. William H. Meyers, "The Hermeneutical Dilemma of the African American Biblical Student," in *Stony the Road We Trod: African American*

Biblical Interpretation, ed. Cain Hope Felder (Philadelphia: Fortress Press, 1991), pp. 46-47, cites particular challenges presented by the dominance of some forms of Eurocentric scholarship as: 1) exclusivity that is inattentive to non-Western and Western minority cultures' hermeneutics; 2) preoccupation with singular orthodox meaning within texts; 3) overemphasis on textual historicity, which challenges the contemporary relevancy of texts; 4) underemphasis on the reception of texts in the interpretive process; 5) inattention to the narrative quality of texts, which results in overemphasis on propositional statements; 6) excessive dependency on historical-critical methodology; 7) preference for passive as opposed to active reading; and 8) attention to a literate bourgeois class while disregarding the orality of minority cultures.

12. See Cornel West, *Prophesy Deliverance!: An Afro-American Revolutionary Christianity* (Philadelphia: Westminster Press, 1982), pp. 15-24.

13. Ibid., p. 21.

14. Ibid., p. 24.

15. These were prominent philosophers of the "golden age" of American philosophy during the first half of the twentieth century.

16. Thiselton, *New Horizons in Hermeneutics*, p. 379.

17. Randall C. Bailey, "Africans in Old Testament Poetry and Narratives," in Felder, *Stony the Road We Trod*, demonstrates how Old Testament scholarship has had a tendency to "deny or dilute African influence on the biblical text (i.e., to de-Africanize) . . ." (p. 168). Bailey cites topographical evidence where scholarship has omitted African nations of Cush, Put, Cyrene, and the like from eighteenth- and nineteenth-century maps of the biblical world; how on other maps Cush, ancient Ethiopia, was located outside Africa; and how modern maps label African territories as "Near East," suggesting that these territories are not part of the African continent. Further, Bailey shows how Western scholarship has created an artificial demarkation between Egypt and sub-Saharan Africa.

Clarice J. Martin, "The *Haustafeln* in African American Biblical Interpretation: 'Free Slaves' and 'Subordinate Women,' " in Felder, *Stony the Road We Trod*, demonstrates how traditionalist and literalist New Testament interpretations of the *Haustafeln* (household codes cited in Col. 3:18-4:1, Eph. 5:21-6:9, and 1 Pet. 2:18-3:7) contributed to the oppression of African Americans in the eighteenth and nineteenth centuries and how these interpretations "concerning the 'submission of wives' in the *Haustafeln* [have] been marked by the marginality and domination of women" (p. 218).

18. Cain Hope Felder, *Troubling Biblical Waters: Race, Class, and Family* (Philadelphia: Fortress Press, 1990), p. 48.

19. Thiselton, *New Horizons in Hermeneutics*, p. 379.

20. J. Deotis Roberts, "Religio-Ethical Reflections Upon the Experiential Components of a Philosophy of Black Liberation," in *African American*

Religious Studies: An Interdisciplinary Anthology, ed. Gayraud S. Wilmore (Durham, NC: Duke University Press, 1989), p. 254.

21. Thiselton, *New Horizons in Hermeneutics*, p. 7.

22. Renita J. Weems, "African American Women and the Bible," in Felder, *Stony the Road We Trod*, pp. 60-62.

23. J. Deotis Roberts, *A Black Political Theology* (Philadelphia: Westminster Press, 1974), p. 46.

24. Vincent L. Wimbush, "The Bible and African Americans: An Outline of Interpretative History," in Felder, *Stony the Road We Trod*, p. 88.

25. Stephen Crites, "Unfinished Figure: On Theology and Imagination," *Journal of the American Academy of Religion: Thematic Studies* 48 (1981), forcefully argues for the importance of imagination in theological reflection. According to Crites, "The primary forms in which Scripture speaks are imaginative, which is not to say that its contents are fictional, but that its primary media are those of the imagination itself: narrative above all, but also visual, lyric-musical, parabolic, metaphoric, and in these forms its figures materialize, materialize between the texts and the imagination of hearer or reader" (pp. 168-169). Further, Crites argues that "only to imagination can an incarnate truth present itself, in concrete figures. Imagination may be false, but only imagination can be true. Theology loses its hermeneutical fruitfulness when it becomes deflected from the imaginative figures presented to it, or even undertakes to replace them with concepts. It loses its essential content" (p. 180).

26. Thomas Hoyt, Jr., "Interpreting Biblical Scholarship," in *Stony the Road We Trod*, p. 37.

27. Ibid., p. 39.

28. Cooper-Lewter and Mitchell, *Soul Theology*, p. 8.

29. Hoyt, "Interpreting Biblical Scholarship," p. 25.

30. Stephen Crites, "The Narrative Quality of Experience," in *Why Narrative?: Readings in Narrative Theology*, ed. Stanley Hauerwas and L. Gregory Jones (Grand Rapids, MI: William B. Eerdmans Publishing, 1989), p. 82.

2. ANTEBELLUM AFRICAN-AMERICAN GODFORSAKENNESS

1. The concept of understanding here is consistent with Hans-Georg Gadamer's hermeneutical approach, which emphasizes openness and engagement as opposed to more empirical approaches that serve the needs and interests of natural sciences. Understanding, according to Gadamer, "does not consist in a technical virtuosity of 'understanding' everything written. Rather, it is a genuine experience, i.e., an encounter with something that asserts itself as truth." Hans-Georg Gadamer, *Truth and Method* (London: Sheed & Ward, 1975), p. 489.

African-American slaves' narratives will be used in this chapter to facilitate engagement with the existential realities of Godforsakenness in antebellum African-American life. Engagement with the language of slaves' experiences allows one to approach an understanding of slaves' experiences as the stories and the reader's horizons embrace each other, yielding a new experience of understanding.

2. The principle source for narratives about life in slavery for this study is George P. Rawick, ed., *The American Slave: A Composite Autobiography*, 41 vols. (Westport, CT: Greenwood Publishing Company, 1972, 1977, 1979). This collection of narratives tells about slavery from the perspective of slaves, a necessary corrective to early studies on slave life that focused on the slaveholding class while neglecting and undervaluing the perspectives of slaves. Interviews in *The American Slave* contradict the propaganda of apologists for slavery who contended that slaves were nearly always happy and content. It should be noted that numerous narratives and autobiographies of slaves and former slaves exist which, in one way or another, corroborate the essential argument of this study and the findings in our body of primary sources. However, these autobiographies and narratives will be used sparingly.

Perhaps the most influential historian on slavery is Ulrich B. Phillips, author of *American Negro Slavery, A Survey of the Supply, Employment, and Control of Negro Labor as Determined by the Plantation Regime* (Baton Rouge, LA: Louisiana State University Press, 1966). Phillips' research was detailed and extensive, but his underlying racial assumptions led him to reach conclusions consistent with the pervasive racist tendencies of his day. Phillips' minimizing of slavery's inhumaneness and extolling of the alleged Christian and civil nature of slavery dramatically distort slavery and stand in stark contrast to the portraits of slavery found in former slaves' own stories. Hence this study will rely on the stories of former slaves to ascertain something of the experience of slavery.

The interviews in *The American Slave* cannot be presumed to be flawless recollections of life in slavery. They were prepared by interviewers—black and white—whose perspectives and biases undoubtedly influenced the recording of data in varying degrees. Further, the subjects of the interviews undoubtedly used their judgment as to the degree of candor that would be expedient in the interviews. Additionally, interviews contained in Rawick's collection were conducted during the 1930s, seven decades after the abolition of slavery. One does not assume that elderly people cannot accurately recollect events of the past. However, chronological distance and the events and information which flow during the interval between experience and interview will influence the precision and purity of one's recollection. Nonetheless, the fact that former slaves have the opportunity to tell their own stories, the thematic consistencies found throughout the collection, and respecting the integrity and recall ability of the former slaves all give ample reason to accept the authenticity of the information found in the interviews. One can conclude that the interviews are sufficiently reliable in general and particular detail for meaningful research into the life and thought of North American slaves.

3. John Hick, *Evil and the God of Love*, rev. ed. (New York: Harper & Row, 1978), contributes to our conceptualization of human suffering. Hick argues that, "by suffering we mean that state of mind in which we wish violently or obsessively that our situation were otherwise. Such a state of mind involves memory and anticipation, the capacity to imagine alternatives, and (in man [sic]) a moral conscience. . . . To be miserable is to be aware of a larger context of existence than one's immediate physical sensations, and to be overcome by the anguished wish that this wider situation were other than it is" (p. 318).

4. Chaim Potok, "Forward," in Harold M. Schulweis, *Evil and the Morality of God* (Cincinnati, OH: Hebrew Union College Press, 1983), p. i.

5. Schulweis, *Evil and the Morality of God*, p. 5. While Schulweis, a Jewish rabbi, is concerned with the "holistic character of monotheistic faith," our concern is with the holistic character of trinitarian theology as expressed in African-American Christianity. Nonetheless, the principle underlying Schulweis' concern about attention to the problem of evil in relation to the practice of faith remains consistent with the implications of this study.

6. Augustine, *Sermo 52*, quoted in Elizabeth A. Johnson, *She Who Is: The Mystery of God in Feminist Theological Discourse* (New York: Crossroad, 1993), p. 105.

7. Karl Barth, *Church Dogmatics: The Doctrine of Reconciliation*, trans. G. W. Bromiley, vol. 4/1 (Edinburgh: T. & T. Clark, 1956), p. 180. Barth definitively argued for the self-disclosure of God in Jesus Christ. Barth's fourth volume of *Church Dogmatics* is subtitled *The Doctrine of Reconciliation*. Therein, Jesus Christ is seen as the definitive revelation of God. For Barth, the doctrine of reconciliation is at the heart of Christian faith and theology. Hence *The Doctrine of Reconciliation* is at the center of *Church Dogmatics*. This theological perspective understands atonement as axiomatic for Christian theology and therefore the only place that allows both forward and backward thinking. The centrality of atonement means that in the sphere of Christian knowledge, creation and consummation are understood as the circumference, while the atonement is located at the center. Further, the key for understanding the mystery of the doctrine of reconciliation follows: The Judge who was Judged in the place of sinners was, therefore, judged in our place and did what was just, thus ushering in a new aeon. See Barth, *Church Dogmatics*, pp. 79-156.

Eberhard Jüngel, *God as the Mystery of the World: On the Foundation of the Theology of the Crucified One in the Dispute between Theism and Atheism*, trans. Darrell L. Guder (Grand Rapids, MI: William B. Eerdmans Publishing Company, 1983), offers a more contemporary explication of God's revelation of Godself. Thinking of God is possible only if one can speak of God. One can speak of God only because God has first spoken to humanity. God has spoken to humanity through God's own humanity, which is declared in the announcement of a new age that transforms the world's self-understanding into a *"change of the ages* and a *turning point in history* [italics in original]. . . . God's humanity introduces itself into the world as a story to be told. Jesus told about God in parables before he himself was proclaimed as the parable of God" (p. 302).

8. Wolfhart Pannenberg is correct in his assessment of human limitations with regard to discerning truth because of the historicity of human experience. See Wolfhart Pannenberg, *Systematic Theology,* vol. 1, trans. Geoffrey W. Bromiley (Grand Rapids, MI: William B. Eerdmans Publishing Company, 1991), where Pannenberg writes: "Solely on account of its historicity all human talk about God unavoidably falls short of full and final knowledge of the truth of God" (p. 55).

9. Rawick, *The American Slave,* vol. 1, p. 125.

10. Ibid., p. 7.

11. John Hope Franklin, *From Slavery to Freedom: A History of Negro Americans*, 3rd ed. (New York: Alfred A. Knopf, 1967), p. 56.

12. John W. Blassingame, *The Slave Community: Plantation Life in the Ante-Bellum South* (New York: Oxford University Press, 1972), p. 3.

13. Franklin, *From Slavery to Freedom*, p. 188.

14. Rawick, *The American Slave,* vol. 1, p. 96.

15. Ibid. Nat Turner, Denmark Vessey, and Gabriel Prosser led slave revolts against slavocracies. For a helpful summary of the contributions of Turner, Vessey, and Prosser to African-American religious consciousness, see Gayraud S. Wilmore, *Black Religion and Black Radicalism: An Interpretation of the Religious History of Afro-American People*, 2nd ed. (Maryknoll, NY: Orbis Books, 1983), pp. 53-73.

16. Riggins R. Earl, Jr., *Dark Symbols, Obscure Signs: God, Self, and Community in the Slave Mind* (Maryknoll, NY: Orbis Books, 1993), pp. 9-23.

17. Ibid. For a thorough treatment of theological justifications in the pro-slavery movement, see Larry E. Tise, *Proslavery: A History of the Defense of Slavery in America, 1701-1840* (Athens, GA: The University of Georgia Press, 1987).

18. T. J. Morgan, *The Negro in America and the Ideal American Republic* (Philadelphia: American Baptist Publication Society, 1898), p. 13.

19. Rawick, *The American Slave*, vol. 4.2, p. 180.

20. Sterling Stuckey, *Slave Culture: Nationalist Theory and the Foundations of Black America* (New York: Oxford University Press, 1987), p. 3. Stuckey contends that this development of unity is the genesis of black nationalism as it would develop in the lives of David Walker, Henry Highland Garnett, W. E. B. DuBois, and Paul Robeson.

21. Thomas L. Webber, *Deep Like the Rivers: Education in the Slave Quarter Community, 1831-1865* (New York: W. W. Norton & Company, 1978), p. 63.

22. William J. Faulkner, *The Days the Animals Talked: Black American Folktales and How They Came to Be* (Chicago: Follette Publishers, 1977), pp. 34-39.

23. Ibid., p. 34.

24. Attention to the "evangelization" of slaves developed significantly during the nineteenth century. This development was related to nineteenth-century American Protestantism and the "Second Great Awakening." Albert J. Raboteau, *Slave Religion: The "Invisible Institution" in the Antebellum South* (New York: Oxford University Press, 1978), explains: "During the seventeenth and much of the eighteenth century there was a great deal of indifference, reluctance, and hostility to the conversion of slaves. (Not until the successive waves of religious revivals known as the Great Awakening began in the 1740s did incidents of slave conversions occur in any sizeable numbers)" (p. 68).

Increased attention to the conversion of slaves evolved on two fronts. On the one hand, some slaveholders considered religion useful in controlling the behavior of the slave population. On the other hand, some Christian clergy and laity were convinced of the imperative of reaching slaves with the gospel. Before this time, instances of evangelizing slaves existed nominally. For example, the Quakers had a history of embracing slaves and former slaves as part of their community of faith, but this movement was not a widespread phenomenon. Prior to the time of significant evangelistic efforts toward slaves, the religious practices of the slaves were significantly those carried over from African traditional religious practices mingled with expressions of Christian worship to which some slaves were exposed. Worship and religious rituals were often carried out by slaves in secrecy, away from the presence of masters and their hirelings. Peter J. Paris observes that blacks generally rejected Christianity for the first 150 years of slavery. Africans had a holistic view of religion and life which perceived religion and life synonymously over against segregating life into the sacred and secular. Hence one's lifestyle was indicative of one's religious conviction. "In short, the slaves viewed the life/religion of the slave master as a consistent systemic whole. . . ." Therefore Christianity was rejected. See Paris, "The Christian Way through the Black Experience," *Word and Way* 6 (1986): 126.

Preston L. Floyd, "The Negro Spiritual: Examination of Some Theological Concepts," *Duke Divinity School Review* 43 (1978), suggests that many slaves who became Christians rehabilitated the corrupt gospel they had received to adapt Christianity to their psychosocial needs without distorting scriptural meaning. Floyd contends that many spirituals are indicative of this rehabilitation effort (p. 105).

25. Lawrence W. Levine, *Black Culture and Black Consciousness: Afro-American Folk Thought from Slavery to Freedom* (New York: Oxford University Press, 1977), p. 114.

26. Frederick Douglass, quoted in Blassingame, *The Slave Community*, p. 104.

27. John W. Blassingame, ed., *Slave Testimony: Two Centuries of Letters, Speeches, Interviews, and Autobiographies* (Baton Rouge, LA: Louisiana State University Press, 1977), p. 169.

28. Ibid., p. 165.

29. Ibid., p. 49.

30. Blassingame, *The Slave Community*, pp. 150-155.

31. Ibid., p. 177.

32. Rawick, *The American Slave*, vol. 2.2, p. 234.

33. Ibid., vol. 3.4, p. 238.

34. Ibid., vol. 2.1, p. 68.

35. Ibid., vol. 16.6, p. 8.

36. Ibid., vol. 8.2, pp. 157-158.

37. J. W. C. Pennington, "The Fugitive Blacksmith; or, Events in the History of James W. C. Pennington, Pastor of a Presbyterian Church, New York, Formerly a Slave in the State of Maryland," in *Great Slave Narratives*, ed. Arna Bontemps (Boston: Beacon Press, 1969), pp. 197-198.

38. Rawick, *The American Slave*, vol. 9.3, p. 40.

39. Ibid., vol. 2.1, p. 67.

40. Ibid., vol. 2.2, p. 63.

41. Ibid., vol. 3.4, p. 10.

42. Ibid., vol. 8.2, pp. 198-199.

43. Ibid., vol. 3.3, p. 194.

44. J. W. C. Pennington, "The Fugitive Blacksmith," p. 202.

45. Rawick, *The American Slave*, vol. 9.3, p. 65.

46. Ibid., vol. 8.2, p. 258.

47. Ibid., vol. 2.1, p. 188.

48. Ibid., vol. 4.2, p. 106.

49. Ibid., vol. S1-1.1, p. 149.

50. Howard Thurman, "Deep River," in *Deep River and the Negro Spiritual Speaks of Life and Death* (Richmond, IN: Friends United Press, 1975), p. 35.

51. Rawick, *The American Slave*, vol. 1, p. 3.

52. Ibid., p. 170.

53. Ibid., vol. 16.7, p. 23.

54. Ibid., p. 43.

55. Franklin, *From Slavery to Freedom*, p. 206.

56. Ibid., p. 207.

57. Rawick, *The American Slave*, vol. S2-10.9, p. 3953.

58. Ibid., vol. 2.2, pp. 120-121.

59. Ibid., vol. 2.2, p. 178.
60. Ibid., vol. 18, p. 6.
61. Ibid., vol. 4.1, p. 27.
62. Ibid., vol. S2-3.2, p. 891.
63. Ibid., p. 719.
64. Ibid., vol. S1-4.2, pp. 350-351.
65. Ibid., vol. 16.11, p. 11.
66. Ibid., vol. 9.3, p. 231.
67. Ibid., vol. 4.1, p. 15.
68. Ibid., vol. 2.2, p. 235.
69. Ibid., vol. 18, p. 136.
70. Ibid., p. 21.
71. Ibid., vol. 8.1, p. 70.
72. Ibid., vol. 2.2, pp. 144-145.
73. Ibid., p. 868.
74. Ibid., vol. S1-8.7, p. 3312.
75. Ibid., vol. 2.2, p. 235.
76. Ibid., vol. 9.3, p. 231.
77. Ibid., vol. 18, p. 44.
78. Ibid., vol. 14.3, p. 49.

79. An important contemporary theological perspective is that of womanist theology. Womanist theology has to do with theological reflection and construction from the perspective of African-American women's experience. Womanist perspective offers a significant critique to the hegemony of white Western male constructions, feminist proposals, and black male liberation theology. African-American women face a tri-dimensional encounter with oppression—racism, sexism, and classism. The challenge put forth by womanist thinkers is for theologians to attend to the experiences of the oppressed of the oppressed—women of color. A meaningful theological statement of womanist perspective is found in Jacquelyn Grant, *White Women's Christ and Black Women's Jesus: Feminist Christology and Womanist Response* (Atlanta, GA: Scholars Press, 1989).

It is important in this study to give attention to the particularity of women's suffering, to acknowledge the uniqueness of Godforsakenness known to female slaves. Sexual exploitation is used in this study only as a representative experience of Godforsakenness for female slaves. To assume that sexual exploitation was the only unique form of suffering would be to assume a sexist posture that values females only in terms of their gender, rather than valuing their humanity. Female slaves faced other kinds of suffering, among which was coerced surrogacy expressed not only sexually, but also in the areas of nurturance and field labor. For a discussion of the coerced surrogacy of antebellum female slaves and the voluntary surrogacy of postbellum African-American females, see Delores S. Williams, *Sisters in the Wilderness: The Challenge of*

Womanist God-Talk (Maryknoll, NY: Orbis Books, 1989). For a further discussion of African-American women's experience in relation to evil and suffering, see Emile M. Townes, ed., *A Troubling in My Soul: Womanist Perspectives on Evil and Suffering* (Maryknoll, NY: Orbis Books, 1993).

80. Williams, *Sisters in the Wilderness*, p. 172.

81. Rawick, *The American Slave*, vol. 16.8, p. 53.

82. Dwight N. Hopkins, "Slave Theology in the 'Invisible Institution,' " in *Cut Loose Your Stammering Tongue: Black Theology in the Slave Narratives*, ed. Dwight N. Hopkins and George Cummings (Maryknoll, NY: Orbis Books, 1991), p. 16.

83. Blassingame, *The Slave Community*, pp. 150-155.

84. Rawick, *The American Slave*, vol. 18, p. 51.

85. Ibid., vol. S1-4.2, p. 423.

86. Ibid., vol. S2-6.5, p. 2298.

87. Ibid., vol. S2-8.7, p. 3292.

88. Ibid., vol. 3.3, p. 195.

89. Ibid., vol. 18, p. 137.

90. Benjamin Griffith Brawley, *A Short History of the American Negro* (New York: The MacMillan Company, 1913), p. 53.

91. Rawick, *The American Slave*, vol. 16.3, p. 34.

92. Ibid., vol. S1-8.3, p. 803.

93. Ibid., vol. 18, p. 1.

94. Ibid., vol. S2-6.5, p. 1973.

95. Ibid., vol. 2.1, p. 150.

96. *Baptist Home Missions in North America: Including a Full Report of the Proceedings and Addresses of the Jubilee Meeting, and a Historical Sketch of the American Baptist Home Mission Society, Historical Tables, Etc., 1832-1882* (New York: Baptist Home Mission Rooms, 1983), p. 77.

97. H. L. Morehouse, "Plantation Life of the Colored People," *The Baptist Home Mission Monthly* 16 (March 1894): 87.

98. *Baptist Home Missions in North America*, p. 402.

99. Rawick, *The American Slave*, vol. 2.1, p. 125.

100. Ibid., p. 342.

101. Letter to Baptist Home Mission Corresponding Secretary from Joanna P. Moore (Valley Forge, PA: The Biographical File of Joanna P. Moore, American Baptist Historical Society Archives, 1913).

102. Mrs. John H. Chapman, "They Needed a Woman's Help," A Paper for the 100th Anniversary of J. P. Moore's Birth (Valley Forge, PA: The Biographical File of Joanna P. Moore, American Baptist Historical Society Archives, 1932), p. 1.

103. Rawick, *The American Slave*, vol. 18, p. 104.

104. Ibid., vol. S1-8.3, p. 946.

105. Ibid., p. 1052.

106. Ibid., vol. S1-7.2, p. 440.

107. Ibid., vol. S2-3.2, pp. 596-597.

108. Ibid., vol. S1-8.3, p. 1143.

109. Ibid., vol. S1-7.2, p. 730.

110. Ibid., vol. 18, p. 197.

111. Ibid., vol. S2-3.2, pp. 853-854.

112. Ibid., vol. S1-8.3, p. 847.

113. W. E. B. DuBois, "A Litany at Atlanta," in *Darkwater: Voices from within the Veil* (1920; rpt. New York: Schocken Books, 1969), p. 27.

114. DuBois, "The Damnation of Women," in *Darkwater*, pp. 176-177.

3. GODFORSAKENNESS IN AFRICAN-AMERICAN SPIRITUALS

1. The spirituals used in this study for theological analysis will be taken from the antebellum African-American experience. These are representations from the slave era for two primary reasons. First, although the spirituals themselves are not considered the personal property of individual authors with copyrighted protection, some of the compilations of spirituals referenced suggest the pre-Civil War era development of the songs by virtue of the copyright dates of the compilations. Books and articles require time for editorial, publication, and distribution processes. Further, spirituals were cultivated and adapted to various communities over varying periods of time. Therefore, one logically concludes the antebellum dating of these songs. The researchers I have used for resources conclude that the selections I have included are indeed from the antebellum era. I have corroborated these claims by cross references and accept the validity of these conclusions. Additionally, it is important to remember that spirituals only gained popular currency among nonblack people because of the efforts of the Fisk Jubilee Singers who, in 1871, began touring the United States and Europe, singing the songs of the slaves, gaining international renown for the quality of their performances, and raising funds for Fisk University. Finally, W. E. B. DuBois concludes, "these songs are the articulate message of the slave to the world." See DuBois, *The Souls of Black Folk* (1903; rpt. New York: Bantam Books, 1989), p. 179.

For those who would challenge my contention that the spirituals selected for this study are not products of antebellum African Americans, I would suggest that postbellum spirituals reflect themes similar to antebellum spirituals because of the similarities of life that existed for both enslaved and manumitted blacks. Even though slaves were emancipated, life was not appreciably different. A change in the legal status of black people in the United States did not immediately transform their practical relationships with the former beneficiaries of slavery. The various continuities of experience, therefore, do not create a conceptual or theological chasm that could result in decreased viability of the conclusions of this study.

Further, each type of African-American music is a source for theological reflection. This is because of the holistic thought of African-American world-views that generally and naturally reject dichotomies of secular and sacred in favor of seeing all of life as inextricably bound together.

2. James Weldon Johnson and J. Rosamond Johnson, eds., *The Second Book of Negro Spirituals* (New York: Viking Press, 1926), p. 15.

3. William Francis Allen, Charles Pickard Ware, and Lucy McKim Garrison, *Slave Songs of the United States*, (1867; rpt. New York: Peter Smith, 1929), p. i.

4. Lucy McKim Garrison, "Song of the Port Royal 'Contrabands,' " in *The Social Implications of Early Negro Music in the United States*, ed. Bernard Katz (New York: Arno Press and *The New York Times,* 1969), p. 10.

5. Structurally, the 150 psalms are arranged into five sections or "books" (Book 1, Pss. 1-41; Book 2, Pss. 42-72; Book 3, Pss. 73-89; Book 4, Pss. 90-106; Book 5, Pss. 101-150). The fivefold arrangement of the Psalter is patterned after the fivefold divisions of the *Torah*, or Pentateuch, and it is generally agreed to have been established in this form during the Second Temple period, in the time of the prophets Haggai and Zechariah. See Bernhard W. Anderson, *Out of the Depths: The Psalms Speak for Us Today* (Philadelphia: Westminster Press, 1983), pp. 13-39.

Substantively, the psalms give vent to expressions that touch the depths of human experience and reach for the ultimate reality. See Roland E. Murphy, O. Carm., *Wisdom Literature and Psalms* (Nashville, TN: Abingdon Press, 1983), who contends that the psalms express "praise, thanksgiving, complaint, resignation, joy, anguish, trust, and awe" (p. 113).

6. Lawrence W. Levine, *Black Culture and Black Consciousness: Afro-American Folk Thought from Slavery to Freedom* (New York: Oxford University Press, 1977), pp. 31-35. Miles Mark Fisher, *Negro Slave Songs in the United States* (1953; rpt. New York: Citadel, 1981), specifically states that, "True spirituals originated shortly after the chief incidents which gave rise to them had passed over . . ." (p. 185).

7. John W. Blassingame, *The Slave Community: Plantation Life in the Antebellum South* (New York: Oxford University Press, 1972), p. 145.

8. Ibid., p. 137.

9. James Weldon Johnson, ed., *The Book of American Negro Spirituals* (New York: Viking Press, 1925), p. 15.

10. See Dena J. Epstein, "Slave Music in the United States before 1860: A Survey of Source," *Music Library Association Notes* 20 (1963), 195-212; and Levine, *Black Culture and Black Consciousness*.

11. Dena J. Epstein, *Sinful Tunes and Spirituals: Black Folk Music to the Civil War* (Chicago: University of Illinois Press, 1977), p. 217.

12. Ibid., p. 218.

13. Marion Alexander Haskell, "Negro 'Spirituals,' " *The Century Magazine* 36 (1899): 577.

14. Fisher, *Negro Slave Songs in the United States*, p. 182.

15. Ibid., pp. 182-183.

16. Levine, *Black Culture and Black Consciousness*, p. 44.

17. Johnson, *The Book of American Negro Spirituals*, p. 17.

18. John Lovell, Jr., *Black Song: The Forge and the Flame: The Story of How the Afro-American Spiritual Was Hammered Out* (New York: Macmillan, 1972). Lovell's use of the term *primitive* does not suggest a negative connotation similar to that of "barbarism." Instead, Lovell's use of the term refers to primary forms and mores of civilization. It is apparent in *Black Song* that the idea of Africa as an uncivilized continent during the era of slave trading from the seventeenth through the nineteenth centuries is a misnomer at best and misinformation at worst. The West African countries, robbed and depleted of their young, strong, talented citizens during the slave trade, had well-developed culture and customs that supported orderly and productive life.

19. Ibid., p. 16.

20. Albert J. Raboteau, *Slave Religion: The "Invisible Institution" in the Antebellum South* (New York: Oxford University Press, 1978), p. 245.

21. Sterling Stuckey, *Slave Culture: Nationalist Theory and the Foundations of Black America* (New York: Oxford University Press, 1987), pp. 3-97.

22. Lawrence W. Levine contends that "without a specific understanding of the content and meaning of slave song, there can be no full comprehension of the effects of slavery upon the slave or the meaning of the society from which slaves emerged at emancipation." See Levine, *Black Culture and Black Consciousness*, p. 55. One might add that an understanding of spirituals is necessary in order to appreciate theological concepts among slaves.

23. Preston L. Floyd, "The Negro Spiritual: Examination of Some Theological Concepts," *The Duke Divinity School Review* 43 (1978), makes the important point that early studies of spirituals seemed to focus predominantly on the sociological context or the musicality of the songs. Since the 1970s, however, greater attention has been given to the theological aspects of spirituals (p. 102).

24. Olivia and Jack Solomon, *"Honey in the Rock:" The Ruby Pickens Tartt Collection of Religious Folk Songs from Sumter County, Alabama* (Macon, GA: Mercer University Press, 1991), p. xxii.

25. Henry Hugh Proctor, "The Theology of the Songs of the Southern Slave," *The Journal of Black Sacred Music* 2 (1988): 50-63.

26. See ibid., pp. 37-38, for an example of heretical doctrine with regard to theological anthropology.

27. Ibib., p. 62.

28. Ibid., p. 63.

29. Willis J. King, "The Negro Spirituals and the Hebrew Psalms," *Methodist Review* 114 (1931): 318-326.

30. Anne Streaty Wimberly, "Spirituals as Symbolic Expressions," *The Journal of the Interdenominational Theological Center* 5 (1977-1978): 24. A classic example of the double meaning in spirituals is found in the well-known selection "Steal Away." This song was interpreted by the slavocracy as a song about private prayer. However, a second meaning understood by the slaves who sang the song indicated that a secret meeting would be held in a previously agreed upon location where slaves would worship without being encumbered by the presence and monitoring of slave holders or their representatives. Another example of the double meaning in spirituals is found in songs that speak of crossing Jordan River. While the surface interpretation concluded that slaves were singing about crossing the river of death that separated the agony of their present lives from heaven's joys, another meaning held that slaves anticipated crossing the Ohio River to head north toward freedom. Further, references to Canaan as a promised land was not only a reference to heaven, but it was also a reference to northern free states or Canada—a promised land of freedom on this earth.

31. Ibid.

32. King, "The Negro Spirituals and the Hebrew Psalms," 318.

33. Levine, *Black Culture and Black Consciousness*, p. 50.

34. Howard Thurman, *Deep River* (1975; rpt. Richmond, IN: Friends United Press, 1990), pp. 11-30.

35. *Baptist Home Missions in America: Jubilee Volume, 1832-1882* (New York: Baptist Home Mission Rooms, 1883), p. 398.

36. *Thirty-Second Annual Report of the American Baptist Home Mission Society: Presented at Philadelphia, May 19-24, 1864* (New York: American Baptist Home Mission Rooms, 1864), p. 33.

37. Wyatt Tee Walker, *"Somebody's Calling My Name": Black Sacred Music and Social Change* (Valley Forge, PA: Judson Press, 1989), p. 40.

38. Blassingame, *The Slave Community*, p. 146.

39. Nathan Wright, Jr., "The Black Spirituals: A Testament of Hope for Our Times," *The Journal of Religious Thought* 33 (1976): 87.

40. Ibid., 87-100.

41. James H. Cone, *The Spirituals and the Blues: An Interpretation* (New York: Seabury Press, 1972), p. 20.

42. Ibid., p. 34.

43. Nat Turner is a classic representative example of antebellum African Americans whose theological convictions and cultural realities drove them to liberating activities. In an interview after his capture and arrest, Turner articulated his divine appointment to free his people from the "serpent" of slavery. "And on the 12th of May, 1828, I heard a loud noise in the heavens, and the Spirit instantly appeared to me and said, the Serpent was loosened, and Christ

had lain down the yoke he had borne for the sins of men, and that I should take it on and fight against the serpent, for the time was fast approaching when the first should be last, and the last should be first." See *The Confessions of Nat Turner, Leader of the Late Insurrection in Southampton, Va.* (1861; rpt. Miami: Mnemosyne Publishing, 1969), p. 5.

44. Levine, *Black Culture and Black Consciousness,* p. 39.

45. Ibid., p. 40.

46. Harold A. Jackson, Jr., "The New Hermeneutic and the Understanding of Spirituals," *The Journal of the Interdenominational Theological Center* 3 (1976): 48.

47. Anne Streaty Wimberly, "Responses to the Paper: 'Spirituals as Symbolic Expressions': Synopsis," *The Journal of the Interdenominational Theological Center* 7 (1979-1980): 54.

48. Proctor, "The Theology of the Songs of the Southern Slave," p. 52.

49. John E. Taylor, "So Let Us Watch: An Interpretation of Antebellum Spiritual Texts," *The Hymn* 38 (1987): 8.

50. Sterling Brown, "Negro Folk Expression: Spirituals, Seculars, Ballads and Work Songs," in *The Making of Black America: Essays in Negro Life and History*, vol. 2, ed. August Meier and Elliott Rudwick (New York: Atheneum, 1976), pp. 215-220.

51. Cone, *The Spirituals and the Blues*, p. 70.

52. Ibid.

53. George P. Rawick, *The American Slave: A Composite Autobiography* (Westport, CT: Greenwood Publishing Company, 1979), vol. S1-4.2, p. 552.

54. Allen, Ware, and Garrison, *Slave Songs of the United States*, p. 94.

55. Ibid., pp. 30-31.

56. Lovell, *Black Song*, pp. 301-303.

57. Solomon, *"Honey in the Rock,"* p. 99. One might note that "All Time Trouble in My Heart" is a variant rendition of the more popular spiritual "Lord, I Want to Be a Christian," which is frequently sung in both black and white hymnody.

58. Allen, Ware, and Garrison, *Slave Songs of the United States*, p. 55.

59. Johnson, *The Book of American Negro Spirituals*, pp. 140-141.

60. Howard Thurman, *The Negro Speaks of Life and Death* (1947; rpt. Richmond, IN: Friends United Press, 1990), pp. 17-20.

61. W. E. B. DuBois, *The Souls of Black Folk*, p. 184.

62. Allen, Ware, and Garrison, *Slave Songs of the United States*, p. 41.

63. Ibid.

64. Thomas Wentworth Higginson, "Negro Spirituals," *The Atlantic Monthly* 19 (1867): 689-690.

65. Johnson, *The Book of American Negro Spirituals*, pp. 170-171.

66. Higginson, "Negro Spirituals," p. 688.

67. Johnson, *The Book of American Negro Spirituals*, pp. 108-109.

68. Thurman, *Deep River*, p. 34.

69. Solomon, *"Honey in the Rock,"* p. 21.

70. Ibid., p. 41.

71. John W. Work, ed., *American Negro Songs and Spirituals* (New York: Bonanza Books, 1940), p. 146.

72. Christa K. Dixon, *Negro Spirituals: From Bible to Folk Song* (New York: Fortress Press, 1976), pp. 35-37.

73. Ibid., p. 37.

74. Haskell, "Negro 'Spirituals,' " p. 580.

75. Thurman, *Deep River*, pp. 56-62.

76. Ibid., p. 26.

77. Raboteau, *Slave Religion*, p. 258.

78. Johnson, *The Book of American Negro Spirituals,* pp. 78-79.

79. Allen, Ware, Garrison, *Slave Songs of the United States*, p. 93.

80. Thurman, *The Negro Speaks of Life and Death*, pp. 37-38.

81. DuBois, *The Souls of Black Folks*, p. 186.

82. Brown, "Negro Folk Expression," p. 211.

83. Work, *American Negro Songs and Spirituals*, p. 24.

84. Johnson, *The Book of American Negro Spirituals*, pp. 174-176.

85. Lovell, *Black Song*, p. 303.

86. Work, *American Negro Songs and Spirituals*, p. 100.

87. Johnson, *The Book of American Negro Spirituals*, pp. 112-113.

88. Ibid., p. 70.

89. Work, *American Negro Songs and Spirituals*, p. 105. Some contemporary versions of the spiritual "Were You There?" have a final verse that says, "Were you there when he rose up from the grave [or tomb]. . . ." This verse is absent from the earliest versions of the spiritual. It seems to be a later addition to the song that seeks to include the resurrection in the story of the crucifixion. One can assume that the addition addresses a concern to provide more continuity with Christian theological convictions about the inseparability of the crucifixion from the resurrection. While the addition speaks to this theological concern, it poses a somewhat awkward movement in the song. The previous references, "Oh! Sometimes it causes me to tremble, tremble, tremble," are related to the horrors of the crucifixion. Why would one tremble in the same way at the glory of the resurrection? If the tremble at the resurrection was different in nature than the tremble at the crucifixion, there is no indication of such in the song as we have it in its earliest form.

90. Johnson, *The Book of American Negro Spirituals*, p. 73.

91. Lovell, *Black Songs*, p. 304.

92. Ibid.

93. Thurman, *Deep River*, p. 35.

94. Rawick, *The American Slave*, vol. 18, p. 47.

95. Thurman, *Deep River*, p. 81.

96. Gayraud S. Wilmore, *Black Religion and Radicalism: An Interpretation of the Religious History of Afro-American People*, 2nd ed. (Maryknoll, NY: Orbis Books, 1983), p. 15.

97. Dwight N. Hopkins, *Shoes That Fit Our Feet: Sources for a Constructive BlackTheology* (Maryknoll, NY: Orbis Books, 1993), pp. 16-18.

98. This concept is compatible with the Christian theological concept of the perichoretic nature of God.

99. Hermes was the ancient Greek messenger of the gods.

100. Rawick, *The American Slave*, vol. 1., pp. 47-48. It is appropriate to note that Christianity has long struggled with the concept of a "shadow side" of God when considering the place of evil in relationship to God. John Hick, *Evil and the God of Love*, rev. ed. (New York: Harper & Row, 1978) analyzes two contrasting views on evil in Christian tradition. Augustine's viewpoint understands evil as a diminution of God, thus having no independent ontology. Irenaeus' approach has an eschatalogical reference in which God will ultimately bring good out of the dark mystery of evil. For the most part, subsequent efforts of Western Christian theology refer to these approaches or variations of them.

101. Jürgen Moltmann, *The Trinity and the Kingdom: The Doctrine of God* (London: SCM Press Ltd., 1981).

102. It is significant to note that the concept of coexistence of good and evil identified here does not go as far as theologies that assign an integral redemptive significance to evil and suffering. Seeing a need to move in a direction other than classical theology's conceptualizations of *Summum Bonum*—the absolute perfection and goodness of God—and *privatio boni*—evil has no ontological substance of its own, but it is a diminution of good—Jim Garrison, *The Darkness of God: Theology after Hiroshima* (London: SCM Press Ltd., 1982), identifies another model of the doctrine of God that he feels is demanded by modern technology's ability to annihilate species of life on earth.

The horrendous tragedy of Hiroshima demands, according to Garrison, another approach to understanding God by all the survivors of Hiroshima—the *hibakusha*, "explosion affected persons" (p. 203). Essentially, Garrison contends that God's self-actualization is realized as God participates in a co-creative partnership with humanity. Since human agents created the destruction realized in Hiroshima, God was a participant. Ultimately, God used Hiroshima and the tragedies of humanity inflicted on creation as God works redemptively for the reconciliation of humanity. Thus God uses evil, suffering, and human tragedy as instruments through which to bring God's will to pass.

Garrison's proposal far exceeds the conclusions one can reach in considering the African influence on slave thought that held good and evil in relationship with each other. Instead, the research in this study leads me to the conclusion that antebellum African-American theology tends toward an Augustinian view (evil as diminution of good) as opposed to an Irenaean outlook (eschatologically, human suffering will be justified). "God, it is true," says Augustine, "foresaw the evil that man [sic] would do (foreseeing it, of course, He [sic] did not force man to it), but at the same time He knew the good that He would Himself make come out of it." See Saint Augustine, "Admonition and Grace," trans. John Courtney Murray, S. J., in *Writings of Saint Augustine*, eds. Ludwig Schopp, et al. (New York: CIMA Publishing, 1947), p. 290.

103. Elizabeth A. Johnson, *She Who Is: The Mystery of God in Feminist Discourse* (New York: Crossroads, 1992), p. 264.

104. Eberhard Jüngel, *God as the Mystery of the World: On the Foundation of the Theology of the Crucified One in the Dispute between Theism and Atheism*, trans. Darrell L. Guder (Grand Rapids, MI: William B. Eerdmans Publishing Company, 1983).

105. Ibid., pp. 43-104.

106. Ibid., p. 62.

107. Wolfhart Pannenberg, "Speaking about God in the Face of Atheist Criticism," in *The Idea of God and Human Freedom*, trans. R. A. Wilson (Philadelphia: Westminster Press, 1973), p. 112.

108. Edward Schillebeeckx's hermeneutic prohibits the conclusion that either Jesus was forsaken by God or that God suffered with Jesus, because the identity of Jesus is born from a Jewish pietistic concept that the righteous suffer for God. Hence the suffering of Jesus was consistent with Jewish piety, as opposed to being related to abandonment by God. Further, Jesus' identity is rooted in his *Abba* relationship to God, who turns to Jesus and identifies Jesus as Son. Jesus, in turn, turns to God, identifying God as Father through the intimacy of their relationship. See Edward Schillebeeckx, *Jesus: An Experiment in Christology*, trans. Hubert Hoskins (New York: Crossroad, 1991).

109. Wolfhart Pannenberg understands Jesus' death as something that happened to Jesus, and it is not understood to be of Jesus' own initiative in the same sense as his activity related to the announcement of the nearness of the kingdom of God. In the crucifixion, parts of Jewish pietism are done away with, and the tragedy of the crucifixion is laid on Jesus. Godforsakenness in this theology is in the death that God allows Jesus to experience as substitutionary for blasphemous humanity. Hence Jesus is forsaken by God, but the forsakenness of death is overcome in the resurrection. Further, because theology is done in the horizon of human historicity, we cannot attribute suffering to God. See Wolfhart Pannenberg, *Jesus—God and Man*, trans. Lewis L. Wilkins and Duane A. Priebe (Philadelphia: Westminster Press, 1977).

110. In Jürgen Moltmann's theology, Godforsakenness is the final experience of God that is endured by the crucified Jesus because Jesus was always cognizant of the reality that he was God's son. The suffering of Jesus was the apocalyptic suffering for the world, out of which God brings good. The Godforsakenness of Jesus here is in the surrender of the Son, wherein the Father

also surrenders the Father's self to suffer the infinite pain of love. Hence the Father's self-communicating love becomes the Father's pain. On the cross, while the godless death of Jesus separates the Father from the Son, the Holy Spirit maintains the bond between Father and Son on the cross. Through the surrender of the Son and the Father on the cross, the Father's love does, gives, and suffers everything on behalf of lost humanity. See Jürgen Moltmann, *The Way of Jesus Christ: Christology in Messianic Dimensions*, trans. Margaret Kohl (New York: HarperCollins, 1990).

Eberhard Jüngel contends that the Godforsakenness of Jesus has to do with the Jewish concept that death on a cross was accursed according to the law. That Jesus' commitment to love was higher than his commitment to the law made him become cursed. Hence the crucifixion of Jesus as a criminal was Godforsakenness. Further, God's self-differentiation allows God to define Godself through God's self-identification with the dead Jesus. Thus the love of God is revealed, in that it gives itself up to the death of the beloved of God. God participates in the death of Jesus and therefore suffers with Jesus. See Jüngel, *God as Mystery of the World*.

4. THE GODFORSAKENNESS OF JESUS IN MARK'S GOSPEL

1. R. Alan Culpepper, "The Passion and Resurrection in Mark," *Review and Expositor* 75 (1978): 583-584.

2. Robert C. Tannehill, "The Disciples in Mark: The Function of a Narrative Role," *Journal of Religion* 57 (1977): 393.

3. Ibid.

4. David Rhoads and Donald Michie, *Mark as Story: An Introduction to the Narrative of a Gospel* (Philadelphia: Fortress Press, 1982), pp. 122-129.

5. Theodore J. Weeden, Sr., *Mark—Traditions in Conflict* (Philadelphia: Fortress Press, 1971), pp. 50-51.

6. Werner H. Kelber, *Mark's Story of Jesus* (Philadelphia: Fortress Press, 1979), p. 42.

7. Ibid., p. 31.

8. I have elected to consider Mark 14:1 as the beginning point of the passion-resurrection narrative, in agreement with the analysis of Thomas Eugene Boomershine, *Mark, the Storyteller: A Rhetorical-Critical Investigation of Mark's Passion and Resurrection Narrative* (Ann Arbor, MI: U. M. I. Dissertation Service, 1974). Others choose to read the beginning of the passion-resurrection narrative as Mark 11:1. See Eduard Schweizer, *The Good News according to Mark*, trans. Donald H. Madvig (Atlanta, GA: John Knox Press, 1970).

I have designated Mark 16:8 as the conclusion of the passion-resurrection narrative for this study. The majority of contemporary scholarship concurs that verse eight is the end of the Markan manuscript in its earliest available forms. However, there is disagreement as to whether 16:8 is the intended conclusion to Mark or whether Mark's original ending has been lost. On one hand, it is argued, Mark's ending appears to be unlike the endings of other narratives inside or outside the Gospels. This could lead one to conclude that ending at 16:8 was probably unintentional. One can see, however, that the narrative strategy employed in 16:8 is similar to the techniques of 6:52, with its inside view and narrative comment, as well as 12:17, where an inside view and a short final sentence are offered. Thus it is probable that Mark intended the story to end at 16:8. See Thomas E. Boomershine and Gilbert L. Bartholomew, "The Narrative Technique of Mark 16:8," *Journal of Biblical Literature* 100 (1981): 213-233.

9. Theodore J. Weeden, Sr., "The Cross as Power in Weakness," in *The Passion of Mark*, ed. Werner H. Kelber (Philadelphia: Fortress Press, 1976), p. 134.

10. Boomershine, *Mark, The Storyteller*, p. 92. Boomershine demonstrates that the term *pistikos*, translated as "pure," has a deeper mysterious quality without parallel in Mark and impossible to render adequately in English. Further, the description of the woman's smashing the jar and pouring out the ointment is also uniquely communicated.

11. Kim E. Dewey, "Peter's Curse and Cursed Peter (Mark 14:53-53, 66-72)," in Kelber, *The Passion of Mark*, p. 110.

12. Schweizer, *The Good News according to Mark*, p. 307.

13. Ibid., p. 313.

14. Ibid., p. 314.

15. Ibid., p. 317.

16. Joseph of Arimathea, who buries the corpse of Jesus, was a Jew who belonged to a group that was interested in Jesus, anticipated the coming of God's kingdom, and was sympathetic to Jesus. They are not, however, said to be followers. One can interpret Joseph as a disciple. If so, his mention is the only mention of a male disciple in a positive connotation since the failure of the twelve. Claiming that Joseph is a disciple seems an optimistic imposition to rehabilitate the tarnished image of male disciples. They are faithless. The women are faithful. This should neither be overlooked nor overemphasized. This fact should not be reduced to combative confrontations about the superiority or inferiority of anyone based on gender, but it should speak to the legitimacy of female faithfulness and discipleship—with all the burden and benefit that may accompany them.

17. Stephen C. Barton, "Mark as Narrative: The Story of the Anointing Woman (Mk 14:3-9)," *Expository Times* 102 (1991): 232.

18. Andrew T. Lincoln, "The Promise and the Failure: Mark 16:7,8," *Journal of Biblical Literature* 108 (1989): 298.

19. Boomershine indicates agreement with O'Collins at this point by noting that the women's portrayal as consistently positive is seen in the use of the verb *akoloutheo,* "to follow," a word of discipleship with positive connotations toward good action (see 14:54). Boomershine, *Mark, the Storyteller,* p. 240.

20. Gerald O'Collins, S. J., "The Fearful Silence of Three Women (Mark 16:8c)," *Gregorianum* 69 (1988): 502-503.

21. Arland J. Hultgren, *Christ and His Benefits: Christology and Redemption in the New Testament* (Philadelphia: Fortress Press, 1987), p. 62.

22. These Markan predictions and their corresponding references in the synoptic Gospels (Matt. 16:21; 17:9; 20:19; and Luke 9:22; 9:43-45; 18:31-34) are considered by many scholars to be the result of postresurrection reflection. This is a distinct possibility. C. S. Mann, however, concludes that the irreducible basic elements of these predictions can be presumed historically based. See Mann, *Mark:* The Anchor Bible, vol. 27 (Garden City, NY: Doubleday and Co., 1986), pp. 342-346.

23. Peter C. Craige, *Psalms 1-50, Word Biblical Commentary,* vol. 19 (Waco, TX: Word Books, 1983), p. 199.

24. It is important to note here that those who attend to the desolation of Jesus' cry avoid doing so in a manner that suggests a theory of penal substitution in the doctrine of atonement.

25. Weeden, *Mark,* pp. 146; 165-168. See Johannes Schreiber, *Theologie des Vertrauens* (Hamburg: Furche-Verlag H. Rennebach K. G., 1967).

26. Carroll Stuhlmueller, C. P., "Faith and Abandonment in the Psalms of Supplication," in Aelred Lacomara, C.P., ed., *The Language of the Cross* (Chicago: Franciscan Herald Press, 1977), pp. 6-7.

27. Thomas E. Boomershine, *Story Journey: An Invitation to the Gospel as Storytelling* (Nashville, TN: Abingdon Press, 1988), p. 167.

28. Ibid., p. 168.

29. John Paul Heil, "The Progressive Narrative Pattern of Mark 14,53-16,8," *Biblica* 73 (1992): 348-349.

30. Kenneth Grayston, *Dying, We Live: A New Enquiry into the Death of Christ in the New Testament* (New York: Oxford University Press, 1990), p. 223.

31. Ibid.

32. Joel B. Green, *The Death of Jesus: Tradition and Interpretation in the Passion Narrative* (Tübingen: J. C. B. Mohr [Paul Siebeck], 1988), p. 305.

33. Mary Ann Tolbert, *Sowing the Gospel: Mark's World in Literary-Historical Perspective* (Minneapolis, MN: Fortress Press, 1989), p. 283. Tolbert believes that Mark's approach is necessary because of Mark's portrayal of Jesus as a suffering Messiah. The fullness of such suffering is found in abandonment by both humanity and divinity (pp. 284-288).

34. Arland J. Hultgren, *Christ and His Benefits*, p. 169.

35. Alister McGrath, *The Enigma of the Cross* (London: Hodder and Stoughton, 1987), p. 102.

36. C. S. Mann, *Mark*, The Anchor Bible, vol. 19 (Garden City, NY: Doubleday and Company, 1986), p. 651.

37. Joachim Jeremias, *New Testament Theology: The Proclamation of Jesus* (New York: Macmillan Publishing, 1971), pp. 66-68. Jeremias' discussion about Jesus' use of *Abba* does not imply that Jesus adopted the language of a small child who addresses the child's father (although Jeremias confesses to having once subscribed to this notion), nor does the fact that Jesus employs the use of *Abba* indicate his cognizance of a christology of preexistence. These two conditions are significant in Jeremias' understanding of Jesus' use of the term *Abba* and its implications for his self-awareness of his relationship with God.

38. Vincent Taylor, *The Gospel according to St. Mark: The Greek Text with Introduction, Notes and Indexes*, 2nd ed. (New York: Macmillan Press, 1966), p. 59A.

39. Ibid.

40. Schweizer, *The Good News according to Mark*, p. 353.

41. Elizabeth A. Johnson, *She Who Is: The Mystery of God in Feminist Discourse* (New York: Crossroads, 1992), p. 268.

5. IMPLICATIONS FOR CONTEMPORARY THEOLOGY

1. W. H. Council, "The Negroes Progress, A Colored College President Presents Some Facts, The Solution of the Problem Does Not Rest with The Negro But with the Caucasian," *Afro-American Mission Herald* 6 (April 1901): 2.

2. Martin Luther King, Jr., *Why We Can't Wait* (New York: Penguin Books, 1964), p. 23.

3. Marian Wright Edelman, *Families in Peril: An Agenda for Social Change* (Cambridge, MA: Harvard University Press, 1987), pp. 2-3.

4. James H. Evans, Jr., *We Have Been Believers: An African-American Systematic Theology* (Minneapolis, MN: Fortress Press, 1992), pp. 16-17.

5. Nicholas C. Cooper-Lewter and Henry H. Mitchell, *Soul Theology: The Heart of American Black Culture* (New York: Harper & Row, 1986), p. 8.

6. Thomas Hoyt, Jr., "Interpreting Biblical Scholarship for the Black Church Tradition," in *Stony the Road We Trod: African American Biblical Interpretation* (Minneapolis, MN: Fortress Press, 1991), p. 25.

7. Ronald F. Thiemann, *Revelation and Theology: The Gospel as Narrated Promise* (Notre Dame, IN: University of Notre Dame Press, 1985), p. 5.

8. Evans, *We Have Been Believers,* p. 58.

9. J. Deotis Roberts, *Black Theology in Dialogue* (Philadelphia: Westminster Press, 1987), pp. 15-16.

10. Michael Jennings, "History's Truths: Scholar Calls Civil War Key to Understanding U.S. Today," *The Courier-Journal,* Tuesday, April 13, 1993, sec. B, pp. 1,2.

11. George P. Rawick, *The American Slave: A Composite Autobiography,* vol. 1 (Westport, CT: Greenwood Publishing Company, 1972, 1977, 1979), p. xiii.

12. James H. Cone, *God of the Oppressed* (New York: Seabury Press, 1975), p. 15.

13. Gayle Jo Carter, "Tipper Gore and Teens Talk Tough," *USA Weekend,* March 4-6, 1994, p. 12.

14. Ibid., p. 13.

15. Ibid., p. 14.

16. C. Eric Lincoln and Lawrence H. Mamiya identify seven mainline black denominations as: the African Methodist Episcopal Church, the African Methodist Episcopal Zion Church, the Christian Methodist Episcopal Church, the National Baptist Convention, U. S. A., the National Baptist Convention of America, the Progressive National Baptist Convention, and the Church of God in Christ. See Lincoln and Mamiya, *The Black Church in the African American Experience* (Durham, NC: Duke University Press, 1990).

17. Ibid., p. 275.

18. Terence E. Fretheim, "Suffering God and Sovereign God in Exodus: A Collision of Images," *Horizons in Biblical Theology* 11 (February 1989): 31-56.

19. Ee Kon Kim, "Who Is Yahweh? Based on a Contextual Reading of Exodus 3:14," *Asia Journal of Theology* 3 (1989): 108-117.

20. Ch. Ukachuku Manus, "Apostolic Suffering (2 Corinthians 6:4-10): The Sign of Christian Existence and Identity," *Asia Journal of Theology* 1 (1987): 51.

21. See Gustavo Gutiérrez, *A Theology of Liberation: History, Politics and Salvation,* trans. Caridad Inda and John Eagleson (Maryknoll, NY: Orbis Books, 1973) and Antonio Emilio Nuñez and William D. Taylor, *Crisis in Latin America: An Evangelical Perspective* (Chicago: Moody Press, 1989).

22. Gustavo Gutiérrez, "But Why Lord?: On Job and the Suffering of the Innocent," *The Other Side* 23 (May 1987): 23.

23. Adrio König, "A Theology of Comfort," *Journal of Theology for Southern Africa* 41 (1982): 55-57.

24. Sun Ai Lee Park, "Asian Women's Theological Reflection," *East Asian Journal of Theology* 3 (1985): 180.

Index